Better Homes and Gardens®
1990
DECORATING
&
REMODELING

ISSN: 1046-459X
ISBN: 0-696-01890-X

CONTENTS

1990 Decorating and Remodeling presents the outstanding decorating and remodeling features that appeared in *Better Homes and Gardens*® magazine in 1989.

JANUARY

THE MAGAZINE FOR AMERICAN FAMILIES

Better Homes and Gardens.

• DECORATE WITH FABRIC
• TERRIFIC KITCHEN REDO
• REVIVING A '50s RANCH

DECORATE WITH FABRIC

IT'S EASY WITH OUR TWO PATTERNS FOR SUCCESS!

By Denise L. Caringer and Robert E. Dittmer

Artful appliqués create furniture with flair. The project pattern also tells how to make the screen and mirror.

Stripes enhance the table's lines.

The bold floral gives a hand-painted look.

FOR GREAT STYLE, GLUE IT TO IT!

Painted or cloaked in fabric, colorfully patterned furniture pieces are among today's hottest accessories. Bring the look home with your fabric, a bit of patience, and our instructions.

5

TOP A BED WITH DRAMA

Yes, you *can* snuggle under a canopy of fabric—no matter what your bed's style. The elegant swags and jabots of this treatment (*opposite*) are a perfect match for the elegant four-poster. But, as you'll see on the following pages, our canopy pattern package also shows you how to give any bed a crowning touch.

FOUR-POSTER ALTERNATIVES
● Sew a shirred canopy and side curtains, or drape the top with lace that cascades behind the headboard.

TRICKS FOR BASIC BEDS
● "Phony up" a canopy: staple fabric over a frame nailed to the ceiling, or suspend fabric over ceiling-hung rods.

SMALL-SPACE GRANDEUR
● Accent a wall-hugging twin bed or daybed by looping fabric over two or three wall-mounted pegs, or shirring yardage over a wall-hung curtain rod.

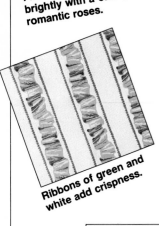

Pink lining contrasts brightly with a canopy of romantic roses.

Ribbons of green and white add crispness.

Free Pattern for Romantic Bandboxes

Take nostalgia to the limit with vintage-style boxes. Our free pattern shows how to cut the box pieces from cardboard and cover them with fabric and trim. Just as in the old days, they'll stow everything from hankies to hats, but, because they're meant to be seen, they won't take up valuable closet space.

It takes only a little fabric to redo a room. Once the canopy is in place, coordinating shams and a balloon shade pull it all together. All fabrics are by Cyrus Clark Co.

Easy elegance frames a bed. The drama: contrast toile with stripes, black with white.

Time-honored toile suits the neoclassic style of the sleigh bed.

SMALL-SPACE DRAMA WITH WALL-HUNG FABRIC

Don't sacrifice style just because your bed is in a tight spot. Looped over two pegs and a towel rod, this "canopy" makes a grand and graceful statement without cramping space. Bold stripes lend snap to the scene.

FOUR-POSTER ELEGANCE FOR A BASIC BED

Is this a four-poster? No, but it looks just as rich and inviting. Fabric hung from a ceiling-mounted frame creates the lofty illusion. Depending on the fabric, this faux four-poster can radiate colonial charm or, using these Waverly prints, suggest safari style.

The small scale of this leafy fabric provides needed "relief" from the large tropical motif.

A bold jungle-print canopy lined with a leopard-skin design sets the exotic mood.

Attach a frame to the ceiling, then add the fabric for a four-poster effect.

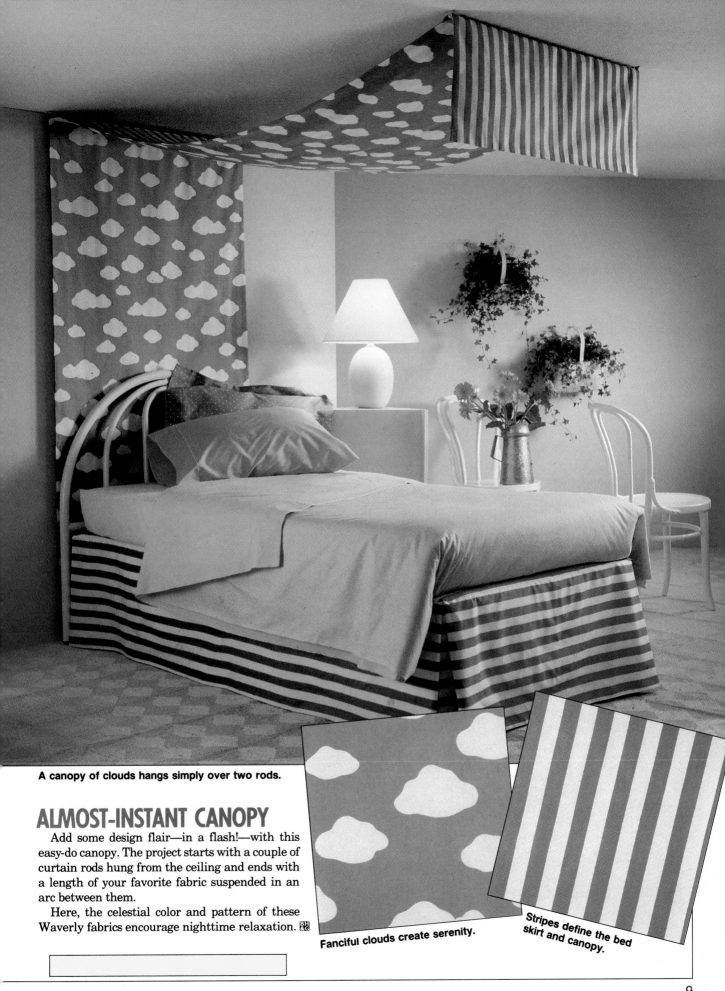

A canopy of clouds hangs simply over two rods.

ALMOST-INSTANT CANOPY

Add some design flair—in a flash!—with this easy-do canopy. The project starts with a couple of curtain rods hung from the ceiling and ends with a length of your favorite fabric suspended in an arc between them.

Here, the celestial color and pattern of these Waverly fabrics encourage nighttime relaxation.

Fanciful clouds create serenity.

Stripes define the bed skirt and canopy.

TERRIFIC KITCHEN REDO
A T-SHAPED PENINSULA LEADS THE WAY

BEFORE

Out with the big breakfast table, in with a cooktop island and scaled-down eating surface. The result: extra storage and counter space. That's just the first chapter of this remodeling success story.

Chapter 1: The peninsula

After their children left home, Karlis and Ruta Grants no longer needed a breakfast table to seat six. In its place stands an island with a self-venting cooktop, oven below, and new countertop and cabinet space on one end. The couple suspended a short breakfast counter between the island and a blank wall, forming a T structure. Drawers hang from both sides of the counter.

Chapter 2: Efficiency

Before the remodeling, the refrigerator and range were in opposite corners of the 11-foot square room. Now, with the cooking appliances in the middle, the work triangle is compact—only two or three steps separate the sink, refrigerator, and cooktop.

Chapter 3: Brighter

Almond-colored cabinets with oak trim replace the dark walnut cabinets, and light vinyl flooring lies where rusty-red linoleum used to be. A new 4×4-foot skylight contributes natural light. The self-venting cooktop eliminates the need for an overhead exhaust hood. To minimize the expense, the Grantses used their own design, purchased stock cabinets, and did the tile work themselves. The total cost of remodeling was about $10,000. 🍴

The sink (*left*), refrigerator, and cooking island now stand within a few steps of each other for greater convenience.

The scaled-down breakfast table (*left*) connects to the back of the cooktop island. Drawers on both sides of the table hold place mats, napkins, and tableware.

● The Sneggs revel in their rural setting. Back row: Robin, 13; Mike, and Nina. Front row: Marc, 7; Alex, 9 months; and Aaron, 10.

REVIVING A '50s RANCH

Nina and Mike bring focus and style to their family living space

By Susan Sheetz

"Our house has all the modern conveniences, but it's still a place where the kids can cruise around and play in the barn, yet be able to walk into town."—Nina Snegg

Mike and Nina Snegg found a gold mine of rural tranquillity when they settled in Nevada City, California. They staked their claim on five lush, pine-studded acres of former ranchland, complete with a horse barn. But before they could cash in on country living, there was some digging to do. They had to restyle a part-of-the-package, ramshackle '50s tract home for family living.

● Gloomy "before."

ECLECTIC '80s REDO
● Touches of Japan, the Southwest, and Frank Lloyd Wright shaped the Sneggs' personal style.

Architect: Steve Brodie. Design: Gary Chapman. Contractor: Jon Klingelhofer. Landscape architect: Josephine McProud. Landscape contractor: Jim Pyle. Field editor: Helen Heitkamp. Photographs: Jay Graham. Food stylist: Stevie Bass

Mike and Nina are self-starters from way back, when they met in an Israeli kibbutz during their vagabond 20s. That same adventurous spirit endured through their travels in Turkey and after they put down roots in Nevada City. Before they plunged into the ranch redo (*right* and *far right*), they had tackled two in-town remodels.

FROM 'EARLY HORSE-STYLE' TO ECLECTIC '80s

Because Nina had grown up in a Frank Lloyd Wright home where the living room was the all-important fam-

> *"We wanted to create an environment that was airy and filled with sunshine."*

● The Sneggs built a new deck and trellised bump-out to improve the flow between the living room and outdoors. The deck overlooks a meadow and a panorama of pines.

COUNTRY LIVING

● The barn's heavy timbers and the sunny meadows provide choice play areas for the children and boarded horses.

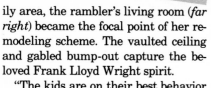

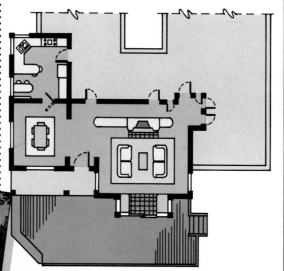

● The plan shows the remodeled areas of the house. "We eliminated hallways and raised the living room ceiling to get a Frank Lloyd Wright feeling," says Nina.

BEVEL-EDGED TRELLIS

● The gabled bump-out's Japanese-style trellis balances a light look with the brick of the original house. The trellis also provides dappled shade from the afternoon sun.

ily area, the rambler's living room (*far right*) became the focal point of her remodeling scheme. The vaulted ceiling and gabled bump-out capture the beloved Frank Lloyd Wright spirit.

"The kids are on their best behavior in here," says Nina. "It's a relaxing place," adds Robin. "You can look outside and see the sunset."

**AIRY ROOM
WITH A VIEW**
● Pushing the living
room out just 5 feet
rescaled the long,
narrow room. "We
added just a little,
but it feels bigger,"
says Mike. A taupe
wash on the red
cedar ceiling
preserved both the
wood grain and the
desired airy
ambience.

13

Marc and Aaron can burn energy shooting baskets with Dad in the barn and cruising around on bikes and horses. "I like this place because it's not too far out of town, but it's not too close," says Aaron. "I can walk to town. And it's very peaceful."

"We wanted a place where the kids could have a little piece of paradise."

BACKYARD HARVEST
● Aaron (*above*) and Robin and Alex (*right*) harvest lunchtime vegetables.

● Low-cost face-lifting tactics like new paint, wallpaper, countertop tiles, and cabinet hardware perked up the kitchen ("Just don't open the drawers," says Mike).

The Sneggs hired an architect, designer, and contractor for this remodel, but, says Mike, Nina was a tough on-site taskmaster. "For instance, she made the crew repaint the walls several times. She would go around with a high-intensity light to make sure the painting was even and the texture was just what she wanted."

A WORK OF ART FOR THE LIVING ROOM

"The fireplace was the hardest thing to do," says Mike of his creative contribution to the project. "I wanted a southwestern feel, the rounded walls. We went through a lot of designs." "After our first try," Nina adds, "it looked like a rocket taking off."

Mike and a friend painstakingly removed the rustic old stones and replaced them with granite tile and soft plaster contours. "It was like creating a whole work of art," Mike says.

MORE CURVES
● Soft plaster contours grace the fireplace walls.

● Sunlight pours uninterrupted through the widened opening between the living room and dining room. The dining room window is bare so the outside view becomes part of the room.

MORE LIGHT
● A central skylight fetches more sun for the living space.

SOUTHWEST SCULPTURE

● The fireplace is a work of art, sculpted with 2×4s, plywood, chicken wire, and troweled-on cement. The recess above the mantel was planned for art. The cutouts in the bookcase walls feed more light into the hallway behind the fireplace.

FEBRUARY

_____

_____

_____

_____

_____

_____

_____

_____

_____

_____

_____

_____

_____

_____

_____

_____

_____

10 PRIZEWINNING NEW HOUSES

NEW TRENDS, NEW STYLES, NEW IDEAS

By Joan McCloskey and William L. Nolan

**National Association of Home Builders
Better Homes and Gardens
Professional Builder**

BEST IN AMERICAN LIVING A·W·A·R·D

Joan and Bill spy a winning entry.

JIM KASCOUTAS

WINNERS FROM EVERY REGION!

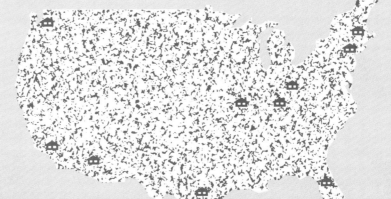

ILLUSTRATIONS: CARSON ODE

WE HELPED PICK 'EM: AMERICA'S BEST HOUSES

Builders across the nation vied for top prizes recently in the Best in American Living Award, a design competition sponsored by *Better Homes and Gardens®*, the National Association of Home Builders, and *Professional Builder* magazine. Contest judges included building editors Joan McCloskey and Bill Nolan (*left*). Join them for a tour of 10 homes that won awards in this year's competition.

Remarkable style and livability per square foot earned top honors for the 10 homes on these pages. Our blue-ribbon roundup exhibits high-performance design ideas from talented builders and architects around the country. Their prizewinners can help you build extra style and livability into your own new home.

Affordable charm in Washington.

High style in California.

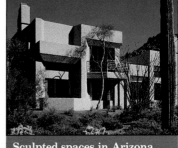

Sculpted spaces in Arizona.

TREND
Faddish design is out; freshened-up classics are back

AUBURN, WASHINGTON
COST-CONSCIOUS CAPE

We start with a show stealer! In this custom-designed split-level in Auburn, Washington, we found it all: charming Cape Cod styling, a wonderfully adaptable floor plan, and an incredibly low price—only $85,000! That figure buys you 1,390 square feet of living space plus a lower level you can finish later as the need arises. Space on the upper levels includes a luxurious master suite, two full baths, and a bay-windowed family/dining room.

Architect: Bloodgood Architects and Planners, PC. Owner/builders: Tim and Bonnie LaPorte. Interior design: Terry Martin for J.C. Penney. Photographs: Bob Strode, courtesy of American Plywood Association

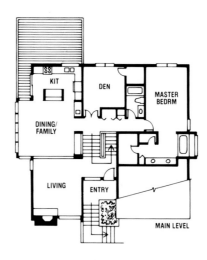

MAIN LEVEL

LOWER LEVEL

▲ The tub in the master bath spans a windowed bay. A big walk-in closet adjoins the other end of the vanity.

▶ Treat the family to a whole wall of windows in the dining area! You can serve dinner via the snack bar.

WHAT MAKES THIS HOUSE A WINNER

- Great curb appeal
- Handy built-ins
- Unusually low cost per square foot
- Cape Cod styling
- Livable, expandable floor plan
- Lots of storage space
- Happy marriage of house and site

The exterior features traditional American detailing that looks at home in any neighborhood: Gabled walls, narrow clapboard siding, and a weathered-brick chimney. The deal also includes vaulted ceilings in the main rooms, a fireplace in the living room, and big walk-in closets in the den and master bedroom.

This house may be just what you've been looking for, but check out our other winners, too; they're loaded with design details you may want to include when you build your new home.

▲ Sidewalls extend as banisters on the deck, making the house one with its site.

◄ What could be homier?—big windows, clustered gables, and a tall brick chimney out front.

CINCINNATI, OHIO
TIMELY TRADITIONAL

It may be more house than you plan to build, but there's design savvy here that works for any house, big or small. Period touches add warmth and texture: wood shingles, Doric columns, small-pane windows, and deep, earth-hugging eaves. A bump-out over the kitchen sink balances tall windows in the turreted stairwell. Wide cornices and trim tie the windows together and set off the shingle siding.

A big wood-burning fireplace flanked by built-in shelving anchors the living room. Stone facing on the chase matches garden walls that border the entry courtyard. Hardwood floors in the main living areas set off classy white columns and white walls. The columns form colonnades that separate the living room, dining room, and foyer.

The master suite adjoins the living room on the main floor; upstairs bedrooms are buffered by a bridgelike hall spanning the living room.

▲ This house greets you with open arms and a lanternlike stair tower.

▶ A colonnade and balustered bridge grace the living room and entry hall.

▲ Windows opposite the colonnade stairstep into the vaulted ceiling. Sliding doors open to the deck.

Architect: John Senhauser, AIA. Builder: Stewart Homes, Division of River City Development Corp. Interior design: Puntenney & Associates, Inc. Photographs: Ron Forth

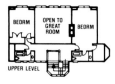

BEDRM | OPEN TO GREAT ROOM | BEDRM

UPPER LEVEL

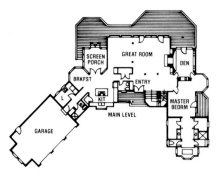

SCREEN PORCH | GREAT ROOM | DEN

BRKFST

ENTRY

KIT

MASTER BEDRM

MAIN LEVEL

GARAGE

WHAT MAKES THIS HOUSE A WINNER
- Deft blend of period style, modern informality
- Spacious living areas
- Good use of southern exposure
- Beckoning front entry
- Good separation of active and quiet areas
- Broad, sheltering rooflines
- Well-placed, generously proportioned windows
- Convenient service entrance
- Sensitive use of simple forms, natural materials

TREND
Smart siting—more
livability on less land

PHOENIX, ARIZONA
DESERT CHIC

Bold planes and airy grids turn this Phoenix town house into eye-catching sculpture. It rubs shoulders with luxury estates along a world-class golf course, but the price is only $216,000. Living space measures just under 2,000 square feet. Looks bigger, doesn't it? Bold geometry inside and out adds heft, and the tawny stucco skin mimics natural hues and textures in the desert.

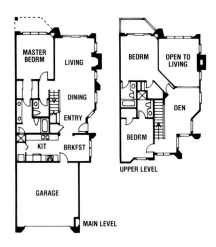

▲Like desert outcroppings, this sculpturesque house fends off the sun with deep, sheltering niches.

▶The kitchen adjoins the garage and front entry. Big windows brighten the breakfast nook.

▲The living room stretches to the roof above a zigzagged plant ledge.

WHAT MAKES THIS HOUSE A WINNER
- Dynamic use of simple geometric shapes
- Big impact in modest-size spaces
- Tasteful adaptation of a regional style
- Efficient room layout
- Streamlined eat-in kitchen
- Handsome shading devices

Architect: Vernon Swaback Associates. Builder: Valgroup Construction Management. Interior design: Victoria D. Currens, Creative Design Consultants. Photographs: Mark Boisclair Photography, Inc.

TREND
The covered porch—a
relaxing energy saver

NAPLES, FLORIDA
PORCH-LOVER'S PRIDE

Taking it easy fits the program in this custom-designed Florida house. The energy-smart plan taps time-tested ideas from early south-coast cottages. Virtually every room adjoins a porch or deck, and the free-flowing interior invites a laid-back, kick-off-your-shoes frame of mind. Deep overhangs let you fling open the French doors to catch a passing breeze—even during a downpour. High ceilings and windowed towers suck the heat up and out. Airy railings let you enjoy the view.

WHAT MAKES THIS HOUSE A WINNER

- Spirited adaptation of a regional style
- Energy-saving design for a warm climate
- Free-flowing floor plan
- Handy access to outdoor areas
- View-snatching doors and windows on all sides

▲ Just try to resist its charms: tall windows, deep dormers, a wraparound veranda, and a turreted corner bay.

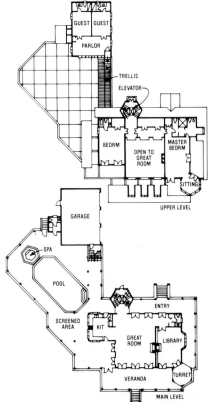

▲ French doors on the main floor open to deep porches on all sides.

▲ Vertical reach and a pale palette add stretch in the living room. A stamped-tin ceiling, beaded wainscot, and tiered mantel with Doric pilasters lend subtle substance.

Architect: Donald E. Flock, Flock and Associates. Builder: Carlson-Harris, Inc. Photos: Flock and Associates

LOUISVILLE, KENTUCKY
BLUEGRASS CHAMPION

Deerfield Apartments in Louisville, Kentucky, harbors creature comforts normally reserved for custom-built homes. You get big walk-in closets, a pantry, built-in appliances, and a fireplace—plus a table-size bar that doubles as work space or a buffet.

▲ The galley-style kitchen boasts two ovens and a walk-in pantry.

▲ This project's porticoed entries take you home to country comforts.

Architect: Reg Narmour, The Architectural Group. Builder: Paragon Group, Inc. Site plan: Land Design. Interior design: Karen Myers. Photographs: Rick Alexander & Associates

WHAT MAKES THIS HOUSE A WINNER
- Inviting, well-sheltered entries
- Crisp contemporary detailing
- Wide range of amenities
- Generous-size storage areas
- Well-equipped kitchen

AUSTIN, TEXAS
VILLA GRANDE

Moorish and Georgian influences give these Texas town houses a dash of Spanish colonial elegance. Each unit sports a rooftop terrace.

▲Fanlight transoms in the living room echo an arched doorway in the hall.

▲The simple stucco forms conjure images of a Moorish palace.

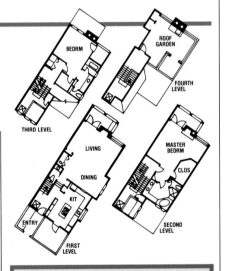

WHAT MAKES THIS HOUSE A WINNER
- Sensitive use of a scenic site
- Thoughtful zoning of private and public spaces
- Picturesque, villagelike design

Architect: Jim R. Nix, Shefelman Nix and Voelzel. Builder: Capitol City Service Corporation, with Playa Development. Photographs: R. Greg Hursley

TREND
Angled views—to stretch
space and charm the eye

ENCINO, CALIFORNIA
CLASSIC CLOISTER

Urban settings quicken our need for privacy and security at home. This space-age house in California updates an age-old solution: the walled compound. Rooms and passageways wrap around a cloistered garden, screening out neighborhood noise and intrusions.

▶ Wings along the lot lines turn the rear garden into a columned cloister.

▼ Stainless steel sheaths a knock-'em-dead fireplace in the living room.

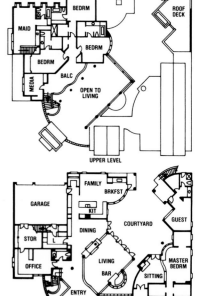

WHAT MAKES THIS HOUSE A WINNER
- Exciting interior vistas
- Blend of architectural motifs
- Intriguing adaptation of an ancient building form

Architect: Barry Berkus, Berkus Group Architects. Builder: Ira Norris. Site plan: Courtland Paul, Peridian Group. Interior design: Nancy Orman. Photographs: Robb Miller

TREND
New regionalism—native
designs retooled for today

DANVERS, MASSACHUSETTS
SUNNY OUTLOOK

Big windows keep this seaside house in tune with its setting. Living space on three levels opens to decks and balconies. The cupola aids long-distance viewing and warm-weather ventilation.

▶ Three levels tap the sun's warmth and sweeping views of the bay.

▼ Kitchen duty includes waterfront views via the five-sided breakfast bay.

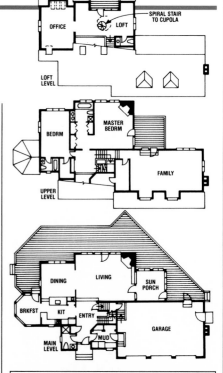

WHAT MAKES THIS HOUSE A WINNER
- Fresh interpretation of early New England architecture
- Solar orientation and view

Architect: Harmon J. Kiley, Jr., Hermit Woods Designs. Builder: H. D. Haynes, Building Contractor. Landscape design: Scott Thomson & Co. Photos: William T. Smith

SCARSDALE, NEW YORK
ROOM TO RAMBLE

Residents at Boulder Ridge enjoy all the roominess and ramble of a spacious single-family dwelling—without the hassle of maintaining a big yard. End units in the cluster shown here feature a pillared entry porch. It opens to a large central foyer flanked on one side by the living room and on the other by the dining room. Straight ahead lies a gracious switchback staircase that serves three big bedrooms on the second floor and an attic studio.

The heart of the house is a big eat-in kitchen with an L-shaped work space and a skylighted breakfast bay. Upstairs, the master suite boasts his-and-her vanities, a separate shower stall, a whirlpool tub and a room-size walk-in closet. The tub stretches diagonally across a marble-sheathed platform beneath a skylight.

Attic space on the third floor accommodates a skylighted studio and exercise room plus two big storage rooms that tuck under the eaves. The studio overlooks the master bedroom, sharing views of the treetops through a Palladian dormer window.

▲ Gables, decks, and chimneys meld Boulder Ridge with its scenic setting.

▶ There's storage galore in the kitchen—plus an island work center.

▲ Ah! Curl up under the big Palladian window in the master suite.

THIRD LEVEL

FOURTH LEVEL

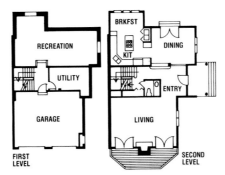

FIRST LEVEL

SECOND LEVEL

WHAT MAKES THIS HOUSE A WINNER

- Handsomely styled and clustered exteriors
- Sunny, spacious eat-in kitchen
- Generous-size living spaces
- Luxurious master suite with his-and-her vanities, separate shower and tub
- Convenient central halls and stairwell
- Loads of storage space
- Gabled entry porch

Architect: Kenneth R. Nadler, Nadler Philopena & Associates. Builder: Ginsberg & Ginsberg. Site plan: David Ferris Miller. Interior design: Clifford Interiors. Photographs: Bill Rothschild

CREVE COEUR, MISSOURI
URBANE COLONIAL

Long, narrow houses needn't suffer from tunnel vision. This colonial-style condo near St. Louis uses height and light to gain lateral stretch in the middle of the house. Oversize windows, two big bays, and a skylighted sun room pull extra daylight into the center of the house; vertical thrust from a two-story great-room and foyer balances the horizontal room layout.

▲Arched windows help snare a lion's share of light in the great-room.

▲The entry courtyard funnels light through tall windows and a big bay.

◄Book-lined walls and parquet flooring add warmth in the library.

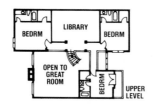

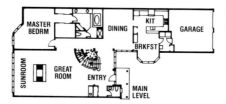

LIBRARY
BEDRM   BEDRM
OPEN TO
GREAT
ROOM
                  BEDRM
                        UPPER
                        LEVEL

MASTER
BEDRM   DINING   KIT   GARAGE
                        BRKFST
SUNROOM
        GREAT
        ROOM   ENTRY
                        MAIN
                        LEVEL

BEDRM   STORAGE

FAMILY
BAR   STOR   LOWER
              LEVEL

WHAT MAKES THIS HOUSE A WINNER
- Dramatic vistas despite the narrow plan
- Adroit use of windows and high ceilings to bring light into the center of the house
- Eye-pleasing traditional styling indoors and out
- Welcoming front porch and entry courtyard
- Gracious curved staircase
- High-quality, well-crafted detailing
- Convenient access to laundry and garage
- Efficient U-shape kitchen

Architect: Richard Just, Arthur J. Sitzwohl & Associates. Builder: Lieberman Corporation. Site plan: Volz Engineering. Interior Designer: Charles N. Brandt of Jack Brandt Ltd. Photographs: Lieberman Corporation

THE AFTER 5:00 KITCHEN

BRINGING THE FAMILY TOGETHER IN STYLE

By Tom Jackson

PHOTOGRAPHS: JIM HEDRICH, HEDRICH-BLESSING, UNLESS OTHERWISE NOTED

Welcome to the After 5:00 Kitchen! *Better Homes and Gardens®* and Whirlpool Corporation joined forces to present this state-of-the-art kitchen that's full of ideas for you.

THE DESIGN TEAM

To create a kitchen for today's families, we teamed up with

RICHARD BRADLEY, PAPARAZZI

the top experts in the business. From left to right:
- Len Schweitzer, Vice President, Corporate Communications, Whirlpool.
- Art Danielian, FAIA, President, Danielian Associates.
- Tom Jackson, Assoc. Editor, Better Homes and Gardens.
- Beverly Trupp, President, Color Design Art.

Mom and dad both have their work and the kids have school, making weekdays busy. In the After Five kitchen they can put meals together in style but also in each other's company.

● TRIANGLE REDEFINED

Try out this two-step work triangle for size and convenience. You grab ingredients out of the refrigerator and from there it's just two steps to either sink. After preparation you're just another two steps from the cooktop. This corner is where most of the work occurs, so we tightened the traffic pattern down to a minimum. With the island and diagonal countertop, however, there's still room for two cooks. The ovens, main microwave, and freezer are used less so we organized them into a baking center on a separate wall.

● WARMTH AND STYLE

The colors for the kitchen were chosen to give the comfortable ambience of a family room, a warm friendly look that's easy on the eyes. The bleached wood cabinets and floor offer the character of wood, but in a contemporary hue. Checkerboard tiles give the kitchen snap and pizzazz. Recessed lights over the work core and paired pendants over the island and banquette adjust lighting levels for different moods and needs. Window views are framed in an eye-catching shade of teal.

A FLOOR PLAN FOR EVERY OCCASION

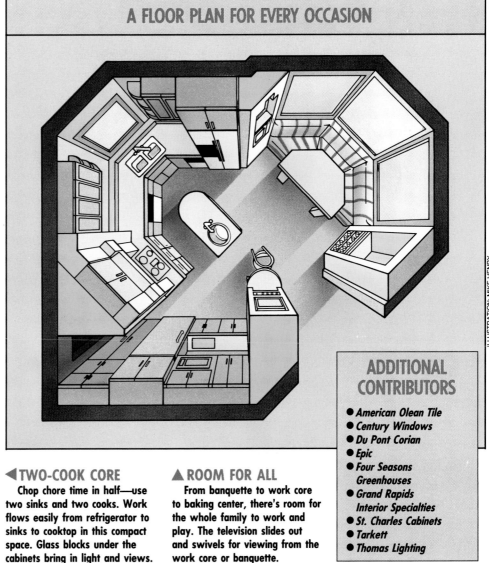

ILLUSTRATION: MIKE HENRY

◄ TWO-COOK CORE

Chop chore time in half—use two sinks and two cooks. Work flows easily from refrigerator to sinks to cooktop in this compact space. Glass blocks under the cabinets bring in light and views.

▲ ROOM FOR ALL

From banquette to work core to baking center, there's room for the whole family to work and play. The television slides out and swivels for viewing from the work core or banquette.

ADDITIONAL CONTRIBUTORS

- American Olean Tile
- Century Windows
- Du Pont Corian
- Epic
- Four Seasons Greenhouses
- Grand Rapids Interior Specialties
- St. Charles Cabinets
- Tarkett
- Thomas Lighting

Base camp for breakfast and the family retreat at night—the secret of success is to provide plenty of tabletop so that eating, homework, chatting, and checkers can all coexist.

● HOME HEADQUARTERS

This is the family gathering center, a place to touch base with one another, plan big adventures, talk about life, or just relax and wait for the kettle to boil. Across from the work core, this arrangement allows parents to be on hand to help with the homework, and the kids are close enough to pitch in with the chores. The baking center (*below*) provides ample space for serious culinary endeavors.

▲ MINI MICROWAVE
A quick-fix for after-school snacks or midnight munchies.

▲ BAKE CENTER
For more elaborate cooking this area offers two ovens, a large microwave, and tile storage niches. A countertop Corian insert is used for rolling out dough.

▶ FOOD AND FROLIC
Home base for the After 5:00 Kitchen is the big banquette table. It's the family launching pad in the morning and a wind-down corner at night.

AFTER 5:00 KITCHEN

DISTINCTIVE DETAILS

▲WINE AND ART

The makings of a small, quiet party for two are never far from hand with this wine niche beside the banquette table. The space above the wine can be stocked with art, flowers, or collectibles.

▲SWIVEL TV

You can see it both ways with this arrangement. The TV pulls out and swivels for viewing from the work core or the banquette. Desk and cookbook storage below assist in retrieving recipes.

▲PARTY STATION

Just outside the kitchen, facing into the family room, this ice maker teams up with the cabinets to create a snack and beverage storage area that puts the basic entertainment ingredients within quick reach.

▲PATTERN AND COLOR

Checkerboard tiles, rich colors, and a gridwork of glass blocks give the detailing in this kitchen a jaunty, upbeat feeling that perks up sagging spirits at the end of a long, hard day. BH&G

BEDTIME STORY

A SOFT-SPOKEN SCHEME WHISPERS A CALMING MESSAGE

By Denise L. Caringer

PHOTOGRAPHS: STEVE CRIDLAND. DESIGN: VIRGINIA BURNEY DESIGNS WITH DULCY MAHAR. FIELD EDITOR: CATHY HOWARD

So, you're all grown up and no one is lulling you to sleep with dreamy tales at bedtime, anymore. With softly colored walls and homey furnishings, your room can give you that tucked-in feeling every night.

▲ Love it? How can you resist. Like a hug, cottage-style wicker, flowers, and glowing woods envelop the room with warmth. Crisp stripes add a refreshing accent.

33

▲ Reassuring ties to the past, the 75-year-old fixtures need only a crisp new backdrop of blue and white to freshen them for today.

► A bouquet of handpainted flowers turns a humble plywood tabletop into an artful accent. Glass preserves the beauty.

When you're homeward bound at the end of a hard day, wouldn't you love to be heading to this kind of retreat? Simple yet sophisticated, this bedroom eschews fussiness in favor of timeless comforts. Imagine snuggling into a thick robe, sitting back with the paper, and nodding off. Cottage furnishings suggest less harried times and places.

The soft touch

A restful color palette, romantic accessories, and a beckoning array of treasured books make every night a happy homecoming.

The right mix

A collection of disparate furnishings creates the look of a lovingly tended family home. Mismatched antique chests are linked both by lineage and golden tones, and a soft spray of white paint turns the metal bed, wicker settee, and bookshelves into a "family."

SMALL IS BOUNTIFUL
HOW TO COPE WITH PINT-SIZE PLACES
By Michael Walsh

PHOTOGRAPHS: JAY GRAHAM. DESIGN: ANNIE BOWMAN, SUNRISE INTERIORS. FIELD EDITOR: HELEN HEITKAMP

VISUAL MANIPULATION makes one room look—and feel—like two.

Even if you can't enlarge your home, expand its horizons by making compact quarters look—and live—larger than life. Here's how.

Furniture arrangements

In small rooms, the first impulse often is to line up furniture against the wall in ballroom fashion in order to open up the middle of the room. But sometimes "floating" furniture away from the walls can be better by:

● **Leaving visual breathing room** around (not just in front of) individual elements to suggest abundant space.

● **Defining space** according to function. Here, an ample white sofa works as a low-profile room divider, giving the dining space the character of a separate, formal dining room.

LOW-PROFILE FURNITURE lets the eye wander to a room's outer limits.

Fool-the-eye design

A small room doesn't necessarily demand small furniture, just fewer pieces. Here, the sofa, dining table, and pine hutch are all amply sized. Their scale alone suggests spaciousness.

Other visual space stretchers used in this accommodating room include:

● **A glass dining table** and slender dining chairs are pieces you can see over, around, and even through.

● **Floor-to-ceiling shelves** make a fireplace wall the focal point, drawing attention all the way across the room and *away* from the space's diminutive dimensions. The strong vertical lines also visually raise the roof.

● **Eggshell-white paint** makes walls recede and maximizes light, yielding an atmosphere that's open and airy.

● **Recessed ceiling lights** stretch space by softly illuminating the room's perimeters. They also serve as out-of-sight task lighting, so that you don't have to fill the space with bulky lamps and lampshades. 🏠

FANCIFUL FURNITURE

SMILE! PAINTED DESIGNS COMBINE ART WITH FUN!

▲ **MOM AND ARTIST**
When it's nap time for Iain and Dylan, it's paint time for artist and mother Theresa Disney.

WITTY STYLE ▶
Iain, captured on canvas at 6 months, smiles at his mom's colorful wares, from furniture to flights of avian fancy.

▼ **FRESH DESIGN**
Bold colors and childlike patterns turn secondhand pieces into three-dimensional art.

By Denise L. Caringer

Is it art? Yes! Is it furniture? Yes! Is it fun? Absolutely!

Painted furniture pieces are hot stuff, and the trend hasn't come close to peaking yet. Here's the lowdown on these high-energy furnishings.

PHOTOGRAPHS: BARBARA MARTIN. FIELD EDITOR: MARY ANNE THOMSON

"When I see a piece of furniture, I look at it as a paintable canvas. I can't keep my hands off the pieces I buy."

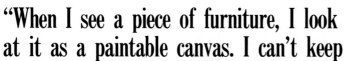

◀ AN EYE FOR STYLE

With bright colors and a touch of her impish humor, Theresa turns has-been chairs and tables into newfound art that's meant to be used.

▶ BRIGHT AND BOLD

What better place to stow the kids' toys than in a playful gift-wrapped chest complete with a painted bow? After finishing the chest, Theresa turned her talents on the used headboard.

Theresa says her house is her studio. In this case, it's a gallery, too. Grouped in the boys' room, Theresa's works evoke the happiness and freedom of childhood. Maybe that's why so many adults are buying fancifully painted pieces for display in entries and living areas, too. Ranging from modern geometrics like these to mellow southwestern motifs, painted furnishings are turning up in specialty shops, galleries, and catalogs around the country.

▲ BORN-AGAIN CHAIR

Because they "looked lonely," in a secondhand shop, Theresa cheered a pair of chairs with birthday suits.

When demand for her whimsically painted birdhouses soared, fledgling artist Theresa took off in search of larger furniture "canvases."

◄ GUTSY GRAPHICS

Mixing the patterns of linens and painted designs creates a freewheeling mood that's just right for the Disney kids.

Inspired? Look in galleries and at art shows for one-of-a-kind furnishings by artists in your area, or try your own freehand designs.

MARCH

THIS YEAR'S INNOVATION WINNER

INNOVATION HOUSE

FAMILY FLOOR PLAN, NEW TECHNOLOGIES, HISTORICAL STYLE

By Tom Jackson

INNOVATION TEAM

The team that brought our 1989 Innovations in Housing to life includes (*from left*): Tom Jackson, associate building editor, *Better Homes and Gardens;* Maryann Olson, program coordinator, American Plywood Association; David Wolfe (top), builder, vice-president sales and marketing, Union Valley Corp.; Wayne Simpson, architect; and Tom Cook, interior designer, associate creative director, Armstrong World Industries.

Come on in! *Better Homes and Gardens*® magazine proudly presents its latest 2,000 sq.ft. package of new single-family home ideas. The cost to build: approximately $45 per square foot. Along with *Progressive Architecture* and *Builder* magazines, we chose architect Wayne Simpson's

▲ Take a glimpse of the dining room from our flagstone foyer. This spot sets the stage for plenty of suprises inside.

▲ A low dining-room ceiling creates a sense of intimacy.

design as the Grand Award Winner from the Innovations in Housing contest sponsored by the American Plywood Association and the American Wood Council. Our builder—Union Valley Corporation of Howell, New Jersey. Our interior designer—Armstrong World Industries, with furniture by Thomasville Industries.

BARREL VAULT CEILING

Here is the heart of our house—a barrel vault ceiling arching above a window-filled living room. While the front of the house presents a fortresslike facade, the living room unfolds much like a traditional Japanese home. Passages outside and to other rooms are recessed behind the stairs and fireplace, and furniture helps dictate traffic patterns.

The slate used to wrap the fireplace crops up again in the entry porch and rear terrace. Just below the cantilevered pot shelf, a wallpaper frieze reinforces the geometric plan of the room. At the

INNOVATION FLOOR PLAN

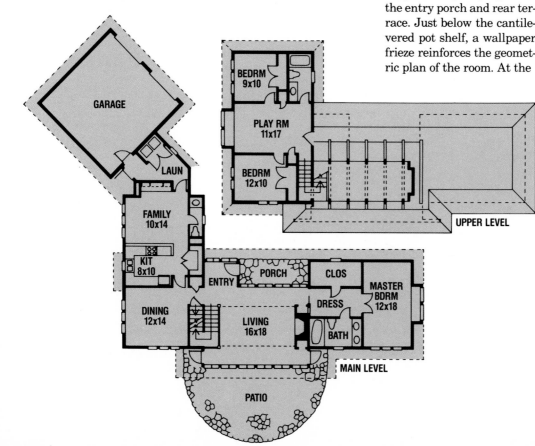

GARAGE

BEDRM
9x10

PLAY RM
11x17

BEDRM
12x10

UPPER LEVEL

LAUN

FAMILY
10x14

KIT
8x10

ENTRY

PORCH

CLOS

MASTER
BDRM
12x18

DRESS

DINING
12x14

LIVING
16x18

BATH

MAIN LEVEL

PATIO

THIS YEAR'S INNOVATION WINNER

▲ Outside, narrow windows and trim create the impression of a larger house.

▼ On the inside, shadows and light mark the path of the sun through the day.

other end of the living room, an oak grill screens the stairwell from the living room.

PARENT'S RETREAT

Slide open the pocket door to the side of the fireplace and step into the master bedroom suite. This series of rooms is buffered from the living area by a dressing hall that is ringed with transom windows. To the right is the master bath; at left, a walk-in closet. Straight ahead is a window seat from which you can look back through the dressing hall and see all the way to the dining room windows at the opposite end of the house. Flat 1×4 lumber is painted and used as trim here and elsewhere, linking the window and door openings with an elegant, inexpensive design element.

◀ With homage to Frank Lloyd Wright and the Arts and Crafts movement, this oak screen elegantly divides the living room from the stairwell.

▶ Transom windows on three sides bring natural light deep into the master bedroom hall from the three adjoining rooms.

▲ A wallpaper frieze above the windows and a custom carpet border on the floor highlight the bedroom's geometry throughout its spacious 10-foot height.

▲ The master bath arch mimics the living room barrel vault.

MIGHTY-MITE KITCHEN

The compact convenience of our hardworking kitchen allows major chores to be done in a minimum of space. To keep our kitchen from bulking up we used some lean machines. The 24-inch-deep refrigerator from Sub-Zero fits flush with the front of the base cabinets, making it look built-in and freeing up extra floor space.

For multifunctional cooking we chose a Microthermal oven and a gas cooktop with grill and griddle, both from Thermador/ Waste King. A walk-in pantry provides storage at the end of the kitchen opposite the sink.

ONE BIG, HAPPY ROOM

The family room is an informal spot where you can grab a snack, read the news, or watch television. Several design techniques visually tie the family room and kitchen together: a repeat of the kitchen cabinet style in the family room media wall, a pass-through counter between the two spaces, and the vinyl floor and wallpaper patterns that start in the kitchen continue into the family room and out into the laundry room. The result is two small rooms that live and feel like one larger space.

▲ Compact appliances and light-toned cabinets maintain a spacious feeling in the kitchen. The counter on the right is open to the family room for quick pass-throughs of food or drink.

◄ For our small-space powder room, this stylishly simple Sapho sink by Porcher provides just the right combination of function and Eurostyle fun.

▶ Our family room media wall locates all the entertainment systems in one compact space.

47

THIS YEAR'S INNOVATION WINNER

▲ Kids can entertain friends, tackle homework assignments, or just relax in their own upstairs playroom.

▲ Low windows and ceilings in the bedrooms create a cozy, loftlike atmosphere.

THE CHILDREN'S REALM

The upstairs belongs to the kids: a separate suite consisting of two bedrooms, a full bath, and a playroom. Giving the kids a realm of their own helps keep peace between the generations. The kids' spaces are at the opposite end of the house from the master suite, so an after-hours rap session or pillow fight doesn't disturb the grownups' quiet hour. Also, the playroom takes pressure off the main living areas downstairs.

ROOM TO GROW

Although it requires more space than a conventional hallway, the playroom earns its keep by buffering the bedrooms and offering a central gathering area for shared activities. There's also a big bay window at one end for reading, daydreaming, or catching up on homework.

COLOR CUES

Teaming the bedrooms with a playroom encourages social skills by giving kids a place to interact and to entertain friends. Our playroom is cued to today's in-the-know kids. Bright colors, jazzy fabrics, and modular furnishings lend playful punch, but teal, mustard, and brick-red accents hold the high-voltage yellow walls in check. The modular units add flexible neutrality—simple blocks that fit the program whether the kids are acting grown-up or just being kids.

▲ Opposite the top of the stairwell, the kids' bathroom borrows bold designs and rich colors from the other rooms in their realm.

INNOVATIONS
Energy, Convenience, and Style

ENERGY EFFICIENCY

Framing with 2×6 lumber allows for more insulation.

Computer analysis

A home with this many windows requires a very strict energy regimen. We chose Owens-Corning Thermal Crafted™ Home program for its tough building standards and computerized energy analysis.

Energy savers

● 2×6 wall framing for an R-19 wall with 45 percent more insulating value than regular 2×4 framing.
● Exterior foam sheathing.
● High-efficiency furnace.
● Insulated crawl space and basement ceiling.
● Owens-Corning Tuff-N-Dri basement waterproofing boosts perimeter insulation.
● Heat-circulating, controlled-combustion Heatilator LX fireplace.

Computer analysis

To determine our energy requirements, all these variables were entered into a computer program with estimates of the average energy use of a family of four located near the New Jersey coast. The result: heating and cooling this home should cost about $830 a year—half as much as a similar home built with a 2×4 frame to code standards.

Deep-bowl sink gives plenty of room for the tough chores.

PORCHER'S BISTRO SINK

has a main bowl 18 inches square and 10 inches deep—big enough to repot plants, fill tall vases, or soak oversize cookware. The off-center drain allows you to let the water out of the sink without moving dishes around. Porcher's Arianne faucet head also helps out with cumbersome chores by acting as a pullout spray.

THE HONEYWELL 2002e

wireless security system can be programmed for full or partial home monitoring. An LCD panel updates you on program status, and tells you where the problems are.

Miele's laundry pair has its own water heater and needs no vent.

THE MIELE WASHER con-

tains its own internal water heater and their condenser dryer needs no venting outlet. Both fit neatly inside standard base cabinets.

Hurd's small-pane mullions echo vertical battens on the siding.

HURD MILLWORK windows

used throughout the house give us the best of both worlds—energy effiency and style—by combining high R-value, double-pane insulating glass with authentic divided lights.

Counter-mounted food center does the work of several appliances.

NUTONE'S FOOD CENTER,

with its motor mounted under the counter, attaches to several stow-away food preparation accessories including a blender, mixer, coffee grinder, juicer, or food processor. Additional NuTone convenience products used in our Innovation House include their built-in central vacuum system, built-in hair dryer, a radio-intercom with cassette player, and a built-in ironing board.

EXCELL CABINETS with

their bleached oak color and simple frame pattern visually tie the house together. To play up the kinship between their deeply sculptured lines and those of the home's architecture, we used the same cabinet style throughout.

Banks of short cabinets form window seats in the master bedroom and playroom; tall, narrow units stack inside a niche near the fireplace; and base cabinets and glass-front wall units house the media center in the family room. The same cabinet style lends period charm in the laundry, bathrooms, and kitchen.

Polished brass from The Renovator's Supply adds period flavor.

RENOVATOR'S SUPPLY

added the finishing touch: historical hardware that evokes the elegance of a bygone era. Our choices include brass towel rods and doorknobs and oversize brass escutcheon plates.

PLYWOOD SIDING with

rough-sawn battens gives our home an elegant look with an economical material. The battens lend vertical stretch so that the house looks taller than it is.

COVENTRY DOORS from

Masonite, used in the interior, are actually hollow-core. These four-panel doors can be stained or painted; they're about one-third the cost of solid-core varieties.

INTERIOR DESIGN elements

play up the architecture. Wallpaper friezes and Armstrong custom carpet borders reinforce the geometric lines. Westgate fabrics in pillows, bedcovers, and window panels, and Hunter Douglas window treatments soften the edges.

LINING UP A LIBRARY
WALL SYSTEMS, BUILT-INS, AND BOOK NOOKS

APPETITE FOR LEARNING. With a book-lined wall, a dining area works between meals, too.

BOOKS ADD COLOR, CHARACTER, AND WARMTH TO ANY ROOM. BUILT IN OR FREE-STANDING, WALL-HUGGING BOOKCASES MAKE THE MOST OF A HOME'S VERTICAL SPACE.

Climbing the walls

Who says you don't have room for an at-home library? You do if you take advantage of vertical space by lining a wall with floor-to-ceiling shelves. Against-the-wall shelving provides storage galore without gobbling up valuable floor space. Besides, a wall of treasured books can be as much of a warming focal point as a fireplace.

Look around your house for likely places to locate wall-mounted shelves, built-in bookcases, or store-bought wall storage units. Dead-end corridors and stairwell landings are often good candidates, as are foyers and under-the-stairs spaces. You may well discover that you have room for more than one home library.

HALLOWED HALL. Birch bookcases, a cozy chair, and a vintage desk turn a hall into a reading and writing room.

Dine with the write crowd

Stacked six high on adjustable wall-mounted brackets, the white-painted wood shelves in this combination dining room and library (*top*) are mounted in a former closet space. Besides corralling books, the shelves also hold stereo components and record albums. That way both favorite reading materials and dinnertime mood music are within reach. The shelves consume only about 7 linear feet of floor space, yet they provide about 42 linear feet of shelf space.

Deck the wall

The truth is, you don't even need a conventional room-size space in order to squeeze a library into your home. Lined with a series of birch bookcases, this 6-foot-wide connecting hall (*left*) was transformed into a functional reading retreat. An ample wing-back chair and an antique English fold-up writing desk occupy one corner and let the former passageway work as a private study as well. 🏠

—*By Michael Walsh*

Photograph (top): Laurie Black and Roslyn Banish/ARX
Design: David and Emily Broom, Broom & Broom, Inc.
Field editor: Helen Heitkamp
Photograph (bottom): Barbara Martin. Design: Nancy Bridwell. Field editor: Mary Anne Thomson

SPARE-ROOM MAKE-OVERS

DUAL-PURPOSE GUEST ROOMS THAT LOOK GREAT

By Denise L. Caringer and Robert E. Dittmer

PHOTOGRAPHS: SCOTT LITTLE

PHOTOGRAPHS: PERRY STRUSE

START OVER WITH NEW FURNITURE

● *Get the most from every inch of space*

ENERGIZE WITH PAINT

● *Brush on some colorful personality*

Z-z-z-z-z.... If your spare room is putting you to sleep, get moving and do something about it. Here's help for two common problems: that catchall guest room (yes, the one with the aging sofa bed and cluttered desk) and the room that looks, well, OK, but lacks *something*.

START OVER WITH NEW FURNITURE

● When home-office needs outgrow your old desk and houseguests look—literally—bent out of shape in the morning, it's time to start over.

What to do? Where to start? A comfortable new sleep sofa can make a great beginning, but don't overlook the alternatives. In this 10×13-foot room, *Techline*'s office and storage components, including—surprise!—a pull-down bed, wrap the room in efficiency. By blending with the walls and fitting snugly against each other, these units also create the appearance of built-ins at a fraction of the cost. Chests and bookcases with optional doors, drawers, and shelves let you customize each piece.

· · · · · · · · · · PLAN OF ATTACK · · · · · · · · · ·

◀ CONQUERING SPACE

To work a lot of functions into a small room—without cluttering the scene—rely on a mix of sleek modular furnishings.

Here, a fold-down wall bed and companion storage pieces join forces with an ample desk and office accessories. The result: a great guest room and a *real* work spot with everything close at hand. Hint: for a sleek wall-to-wall look, position the desk, bed, and other storage units, then roll the "return" (it holds the computer) into place to fill any remaining gap.

NOW AND THEN ▶

What a difference, eh? While there was nothing really wrong with the original, there was nothing especially right about it, either. A case of "brownout" and a lack of personality did little to welcome houseguests or the owners.

BEFORE

▲ PERSONALITY PROFILE

Fire up a roomful of beige and white with bold contrast: black accents, a richly patterned rug, and a terra-cotta wall. For real pizzazz, make something out of the lone window; rim it with a lambrequin and underline it with a sleek chest.

START OVER WITH NEW FURNITURE

To make the most of flexible modular furnishings like these, start with a list of your needs, then select the pieces that will satisfy them. In this case, the owners wanted not only guest sleeping quarters and an ample "homework" spot, but also storage for books, clothing, and a family of rabbits that, not surprisingly, is growing at a rapid pace! When planning your room, consider these small-space basics:

● **USE VERTICAL SPACE** to add maximum storage and a look of height.

● **LEAVE SOME BREATHING ROOM.** Your room will feel larger if you don't fill every inch of floor and wall space.

● **SELECT WHITE** for most surfaces; dramatize with bright or dark accents.

SHOPPING LIST	
Wall bed (double, mattress not included)	$1,140
4-drawer dresser	$245
60-in. desk	$211
Typing return	$144
File cabinet with casters	$192
Bookcase (36"w × 86¼"h × 18¼"d) fitted with 1 shelf, 4 deep drawers, 2 doors	$582
Bookcase (18⅜"w × 73¾"h × 11⅝"d) comes with 5 shelves	$156
Bookcase (36"w × 73¾"h × 11⅝"d) comes with 5 shelves	$204

(*Prices are approximate and may vary.*)

FLASH FROM THE PAST ▶
After falling into disfavor decades ago, space-saving pull-down beds are springing back into action these days. The bed's cabinet bolts securely to the wall studs behind it.

▲ **AN EFFICIENT L** of hardworking furnishings cushioned by new *Karastan* carpet turns a corner into a practical work spot. When guests arrive, the rolling file cabinet works overtime as a night table. Office romance: favorite artwork softens the workaday setting.

▲ **SLIM BOOKCASES** add denlike warmth to the room, yet consume only a 12-inch-deep path.

▲ **BEHIND CLOSED DOORS,** guest linens and a spill-over of clothing from the master bedroom tuck out of sight.

▲ **A SIMPLE WOOD LAMBREQUIN,** sleek mini blinds, and a chest turn the once-awkward window into a decorative bonus.

▲ **PERFECT BALANCE.** You can pull the bed down with one hand. Count on it to hold its position safely anywhere along the line.

ENERGIZE WITH PAINT

● Sure, you want guests to relax, but don't let your room put them to sleep before bedtime.

If the basics are fine, wake things up with some stimulating strokes of color. The essential ingredient: a clear vision of the look you want. Here, the owners decided to turn up the heat on their tepid country scheme with a gutsy painted floor. They finished their redecorating job with clean-lined Shaker chairs and some contemporary lamps— distant cousins that share the same form-is-function ancestry.

BEFORE

·················· **PLAN OF ATTACK** ··················

HOME
WORK
SPOT

SLEEPING
LOUNGING
AREA

▲ NOT BAD, NOT GOOD

Too often, "country" decorating deteriorates into simply dull design. Inviting for lounging and, with the trundle raised, comfortable for sleeping, the metal daybed was a good start. What the room lacked: one bold element to set the mood.

COUNTRY CONFIDENCE ▶

Inspired by a treasured quilt, the owners awakened the room with khaki, red, and high-energy white. The painted floor, set on the diagonal to add an illusion of width to the narrow spaces, gives the room the strength of character it needed.

◀ PULLING TOGETHER

Because the original furniture arrangement worked, the owners did only a little reshuffling, and focused, instead, on sharpening their down-home decorating point. The checkered floor and painted window trim bind the rooms together.

DESIGN SPONSOR: NATIONAL PAINT AND COATINGS ASSOCIATION

ENERGIZE WITH PAINT

BEFORE

Giving the rooms a decorative identity and warming them for guests was only one part of the scheme. The other? Turning the old sleeping porch into a cozy library-style getaway for desk work and reading.

Although the original furniture (*above*) worked well enough, the overall effect was dull, at best. In addition, the untreated windows caused glare and admitted summertime heat and wintertime drafts. After painting the checked floor, the owners:

● **UNIFIED** the windows with paint and *Hunter Douglas'* *"Duette"* shades.

● **ADDED STYLE** with both new and refinished furnishings. 🄱🄷&🄶

▲ **A DECIDEDLY SHAKER MOOD** replaces the once-vague "country" theme. Instead of a museumlike replica of the past, however, this room mixes modern lamps, storage, and energy-wise window shades with antique tables and *Shaker Workshops'* reproduction seating.

SHOPPING LIST

Window shades (honeycomb pleated design)—
   range $8 to $13 per sq. ft.
Shawl-back rocker—kit $157.50
   assembled and finished $305
Side chair—kit. $120
   assembled and finished $240
Settee—kit $237.50
   assembled and finished $475
Round candle stand—kit $63.75
   assembled and finished $127.50
Black bookcases (each). $99
Bed skirt $27
Paint and supplies $249
Floor lamps (each) $82
Table lamp $266

(*Prices are approximate and may vary.*)

▲ **LET THERE BE WHITE!** With its fresh whitewashed finish and decades-old craftsmanship, a vintage library table bridges the gap between the room's old and new elements. Like the artful lamp, the bench combines purity of line with no-nonsense function.

REST-EASY DECORATING
PRINTS AND SHEET FABRIC REFRESH A BEDROOM

A profusion of petals lends romance and lushness to this restful bedroom.

Don't be a wallflower; be free with pattern to create a space rich with style. Given a spirited bouquet of prints, this bedroom has blossomed into an invitingly elegant, soul-soothing retreat.

Melding a mix

Garden-fresh roses, strewn lavishly over fabrics and wall coverings, lend this bower lushness. Take cues from this room to put prints in your place:

● **Pick a dominant pattern.** The strong print in the mix—an allover floral in the duvet cover and canopy—is an apt choice for the focal-point bed. The rose-bordered bed curtains tie in by motif and the canopy by soft color.

● **Weave the style throughout.** Varied and lighter in scale, accent pat-

And in this corner, layers of fabric, a big easy chair, and lace-filtered sunlight pamper visitors.

terns carry the design thread of color and motif around the room, yet don't compete with the dominant floral.

● **Add color contrast.** Dark, leafy backgrounds in the wall covering set off the mostly light scheme.

● **Distribute the pattern evenly.** Garden-variety patterns are planted evenly from sitting nook to carpet, giving the room a pleasing balance.

The price is right with sheets

Dressing your spaces in prints need not be costly, as this setting proves. The look is luxurious, but far from expensive. That's because stylish sheets dress the bed, from canopy to dust ruffle. Smart shopping yielded the wall covering, a designer look-alike that cost a fraction of the original.

APRIL

LIVEN UP WITH LIGHT

REVIVE A TIRED HOUSE WITH LIGHT-CATCHERS

By William L. Nolan

Extra doses of daylight in the right places can make your house look newer, bigger, more dramatic. Check out the stylish daylighting ploys on these pages. They show you how to make dark corners come to life and turn ho-hum rooms into favorite retreats.

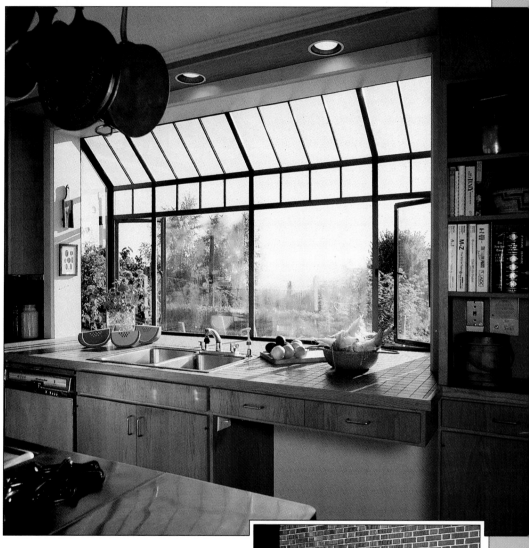

COUNTERTOP BAY

● *The sink in this kitchen is almost outdoors! An oversize greenhouse bump-out at countertop height scoops in limitless horizons and loads of light.*

▲ **INTERIOR**

This 18-inch-deep greenhouse bump-out brightens the whole kitchen—and makes it seem twice as big!

▶ **EXTERIOR**

The owners had the factory size up a standard greenhouse bay. Extra metal strips lend a leaded-glass effect.

ARCHITECT: TED GRANGER. PHOTOGRAPHS: MIKE JENSEN
FIELD EDITOR: TRISH MAHARAM

SKYLIGHTED DORMER

● *This glass-topped dormer shunts light to the living room and upstairs hall.*

▶ **EXTERIOR**

The dormer's skylight and side windows grab extra light. Cape Cod styling merges dormer and house.

▼ **INTERIOR**

Light spills down the back wall of the living room, dramatizing the high ceiling and carved mantel.

ARCHITECT: JIM MACDONALD. PHOTOGRAPHS: JAY GRAHAM. FIELD EDITOR: HELEN HEITKAMP

ARCHITECT: GEORGE MIERS & ASSOCIATES. PHOTOGRAPHS: JAY GRAHAM. FIELD EDITOR: HELEN HEITKAMP

TRANSOM CUTOUTS

● *Even small doses of light lend oomph. Here, extra openings near the ceiling boost the brightness—while adding some eye-catching punch.*

▲ INTERIOR

Shapely transoms help mate this family/dining room addition with the garden. The transoms point up the high ceiling; white walls spread the light.

▶ EXTERIOR

Simple cutouts near the eaves snare extra light and view. Their classic geometry nods to Georgian styling out front.

BREAKFAST BAY

● *A wide arch and sunny bay give this once-windowless kitchen a fresh outlook.*

▼ INTERIOR

A dreary mudroom once kept this kitchen in the dark. Now the sun pours in all day—even through the ceiling!

▶ EXTERIOR

Square-mullioned transoms stretch this bay window to the eaves. The skylight matches the width of the front opening. 🔳

ARCHITECT: CLAYTON O'BRIEN-SMITH, GGLO ARCHITECTURE GROUP. PHOTOGRAPHS: MIKE JENSEN. FIELD EDITOR: TRISH MAHARAM.

LIZ AND PETER ROBINSON

FARM-FRESH STYLE

The Robinsons revive a rural Seattle home with a loving touch

By Sandra Soria and
Douglas A. Jimerson

Go over the water and through the woods and you'll arrive at Liz and Peter Robinson's home. The crunch of tires on gravel greets all who roll onto the two acres—signaling that the past hasn't been paved over in favor of the present here.

PHOTOGRAPHS: MIKE JENSEN. FIELD EDITOR: TRISH MAHARAM

"The house and garden certainly didn't look this way when we began . . . Peter and I made them proud again."

—Liz

▲ SOFT SCENTS, BRIGHT SIGHTS
Blooming vines, bushes, and flowers bid welcome.

◄ A FRIENDLY MIX OF OBJECTS
Family items and gems found along the way warm this home.

Perched on a hill on Seattle's Bainbridge Island, this 1895 farmhouse stands like a monument to the grace and simplicity of days gone by. Getting it into farm-fresh condition, though, proved to be a monumental task.

When the couple bought the home four years ago, it

> "I believe that if you love something—a child, a house, an animal—it will reflect that."
>
> —Liz

needed a lot of attention. More attention, really, than Peter—a computer specialist—wanted to give it.

"When I first saw this house," Peter recalls, "I said, 'No way, Elizabeth!' Eventually, I calmed down and began to share her vision."

Liz saw the shabby structure and overgrown gardens as a likely spot to indulge her passion for gardening and decorating, and Peter's love of woodworking. "I felt sorry for the house," says the homemaker. "It didn't deserve that kind of neglect."

Although major redos (such as scraping linoleum and black adhesive from the original fir floors) were left to experts, the Robinsons revived much of the home with their own handy hands.

With Peter wielding the hammer, Liz pushing the paintbrush, and their five grown children pitching in when possible, the renovation became a true family affair. By doing a lot of the work, the family could thrill at uncovering the home's unique character bit by bit.

▲ **GRAND ENTRANCE** Peter nailed on siding and Liz pasted on wall covering to brighten the foyer. "We chose fruit paper because the yard is full of fruit trees," says Liz. "It makes a nice greeting."

▲ **NO PLACE LIKE IT** Being able to relax in the charming setting they created together is the reward for Liz and Peter.

FARM-FRESH STYLE

Downstairs, stripping off layers of wallpaper revealed wide, ship's-plank walls. "It was like discovering buried treasure," Liz recalls.

> "Liz tells me I'm a good fixer-upper. I guess when you have five kids, you learn to do things so you don't have to pay anyone else to do them."
> —Peter

Like the old-time architecture, vintage furnishings warm the home. Some pieces have lived with Liz and Peter for years, others have been inherited, still others are adopted castoffs.

Built on a sturdy foundation of memories, this house radiates warmth even on the dampest Seattle days. Maybe that's why the Robinson children ("I still can't believe they're grown!" Liz groans) find reasons other than ma-

▲ **FAMILY GATHERING** The Robinson children escape city digs to rest and relax at their parents' rural residence. Pictured from left to right: Paul, Susan, Liz, Gretchen, Peter, Barbara (not shown, Mark).

▲ **Robust raspberry paint perks up old wicker.**

jor holidays to gather round. The deck that Peter built provides an ample area for impromptu family reunions.

▲ **MIXED COMPANY** This dining room gets personality from a varied guest list, including a pine table, Liz's Grandma's oak dining chairs, old-favorite wing chairs, and scrolls from Liz's childhood in China.

▲ **HOT COFFEE AND WARM CONVERSATION**
These are always in supply at the Robinsons'. A handy island lets Liz catch up with friends while she cooks. Overhead, a pot rack keeps cookware at arm's length. "Peter built it. Now I don't make as much noise," Liz quips.

FARM-FRESH STYLE

A steep climb up the back stairwell from the kitchen reveals a trio of second-floor bedrooms. These cozy nooks offer ready havens when the family gatherings evolve unexpectedly into slumber parties. Once a labyrinth of tiny, dark spaces, the rooms owe their breezy country charm to the magic of paint.

"It's amazing what a lot of sanding and a little paint can do," says Liz. "The bedroom floors were in bad shape. But we didn't want to call the workers back, so we sanded away and splashed on industrial floor paint. Turns out, these floors are easier to keep up than the finished floor downstairs."

In these rooms, and in most every room in the house, paint adds personality. "My daughter, Barbara,

> "All the colors in our home were picked from the garden. I thought that way they would look natural and flow like a dream."
> —Liz

helps me paint," Liz explains. "When we were doing these rooms, we were just getting puffed up with our proficiency at painting and making stencils—so we put them everywhere!"

Peter added architectural character to the bedrooms by nailing on wainscots. "I don't think I'm particularly skilled at carpentry," shrugs a modest Peter, "but I enjoy it." For Peter, it's a great way to downshift to a slower pace after a hectic week of work at a Seattle bank.

▲ **HANG UPS**
On a pegged board, Liz's infant clothing hangs like a mural of memories.

◄ **IMPORTED IDEA**
"My sister used to live in Europe," says Liz, "and every bedroom had a sink. It charmed me."

▼ **BOOK NOOK**
This vintage home has built-in character.

"I asked my daughter Susan what color she'd paint this room," explains Liz, "and she blurted 'Yellow!' Now I walk in and think of her—she's light-hearted and happy, too." A checkerboard floor and winding stenciled border add to the relaxed mood.

Vintage fixtures, a checkerboard of resilient tiles, and watercolor-soft hues turn on the charm in the master bath. "I thought Peter and our boys were going to faint when I asked them to haul that tub in from the backyard," Liz recalls with a smile.

Simple pleasures make this home special. Indeed, pedigree is never the point here. Most objects—even the home itself—have humble beginnings. But when Peter and Liz turn their attention to something, the object gets a second chance.

"Our most prized furniture is basically junk that we've spent hours refinishing," confirms Liz. Case in point: the clawfoot tub and farm sink in the couple's master bath were both found in backyard sheds. Peter and sons hauled them indoors, Liz sanded the rust-clad pieces, then they called a local refinisher to revive them with fresh enamel.

In the Robinson home, vintage elements, such as the fixtures or the passed-down quilt that dresses the couple's bed, are always put to use rather than put out to pasture. By making them a part of their everyday lives, the Robinsons turn the objects into living tributes to yesterday's grace, not simply ghosts from the past.

> "Being in this house is like being read to. Everywhere I look takes me back, because every object tells a story about our family history."
> —Liz

While she gathers and displays yesterday's treasures, Liz is also busy creating tomorrow's heirlooms. Besides perking up walls and floors with stenciled-on patterns, Liz also makes paint projects "to go." She's dabbled in various stenciled fabrics, such as the canvas floorcloth she's working on (*right*), which she offers as gifts to family and friends.

"Barbara and I learned the basics from a magazine article a few years ago," Liz comments. "Now we don't follow directions; we design a lot of our own patterns."

Appended to the home's south side, the solarium is an inspirational studio for Liz's creative projects. From here she can take in the lush countryside, or monitor the garden's blossoms.

"These windows frame a wonderful, seasonal picture," Liz comments. "On sunny winter days the solarium heats the whole house."

▲ SETTING SIGHTS

Wispy lace panels soften the master bedroom's bow window and frame a favorite view of the Robinson acres. "We don't have a lot of land," says Peter, "but it's nice to have a buffer of green—room to spread out."

▶ PRACTICAL PASTIME

Liz personalizes her home's interiors—and even creates gifts—with her stencil skills.

MAY

THE MAGAZINE FOR AMERICAN FAMILIES

Better Homes and Gardens

- *WHAT YOU WANT IN A NEW HOME TODAY*
- *AFFORDABLE STYLE*

① **Eye-catching exterior**

● Jack Bloodgood designed this house in conjunction with *Better Homes and Gardens*® magazine and the builder, Hometime, for a recent 10-part public television series, *Contracting Your Own Home*. See how the house reflects Jack's 10 essentials for good design on the next 8 pages.

BY
SUSAN SHEETZ

WHAT YOU WANT IN A
NEW HOME TODAY

AMERICA'S TOP FAMILY-HOME AND AWARD-WINNING ARCHITECT SHARES HIS ELEMENTS OF GOOD DESIGN

Jack Bloodgood

John D. (Jack) Bloodgood, is a former building editor of *Better Homes and Gardens* magazine. He is president of Bloodgood Architects & Planners, Inc., P.C., a national architectural firm with offices in Des Moines, Boston, and Tampa.

10 ESSENTIALS FOR GOOD HOME DESIGN

① **Eye-catching exterior.** Houses should project an air of substance and architectural richness.

② **Entry excitement.** When entering, guests should get a sense of depth by being able to catch glimpses into nearby rooms.

③ **Through-views.** Homeowners should be able to look from one space into another or beyond through windows, wall cutouts, and glass doors.

④ **Volumetrics.** Ceilings are on the rise, and they're vaulted, trayed—interesting!

⑤ **Zoning.** The kitchen, breakfast room, and family room work together but are separate spaces in one main area.

⑥ **Master suite excitement.** Couples want a spacious showcase setting for relaxing, refreshening, and exercising.

⑦ **Indoor/outdoor orientation.** Lots of rooms with a view and outside access merge indoor and outdoor living spaces.

⑧ **Strategic storage.** Useful built-ins and closets should provide convenient places to store items so they're easy to get at and to keep organized.

⑨ **Architectural detailing, inside and out.** Nice exterior finishes and style should carry all the way through.

⑩ **Lots of light.** More at-home activities demand extra ceiling, built-in, and natural lighting.

U sing the Hometime house, Jack explains how the changing needs of today's families have affected his new-home designs.

SOPHISTICATED BUYERS

Today's home buyers are a group of sophisticated, knowledgeable consumers. These move-up buyers, executive families, and growing mid-life families want to be part of the American success. And they want their houses to reflect that. Their

Owners want the inside contemporary and relaxed—providing easy living and maintenance.

houses should project an air of substance and architectural richness.

Inside, though, they want a house that is contemporary and relaxed—providing easy living and maintenance. The trend is toward an informal lifestyle with the family and entertaining at home. The house we designed for Hometime (*above and right*) is a good example.

1 Eye-catching exterior **9** Architectural detailing

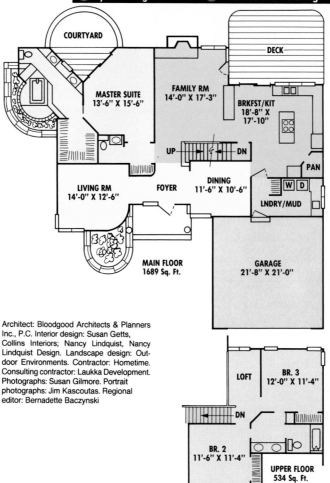

Architect: Bloodgood Architects & Planners Inc., P.C. Interior design: Susan Getts, Collins Interiors; Nancy Lindquist, Nancy Lindquist Design. Landscape design: Outdoor Environments. Contractor: Hometime. Consulting contractor: Laukka Development. Photographs: Susan Gilmore. Portrait photographs: Jim Kascoutas. Regional editor: Bernadette Baczynski

▲ Although the house is a story-and-a-half, interesting massing of textured materials and simple overframing create the effect of a soaring two-story. Cedar shake siding and shingles blend the home with its wooded lot. Brick accents and highlights the steps, planters, columns, and garage walls.

5 Zoning

◀ The living and dining rooms function quietly out of the main traffic flow. Open planning lets your clan get together in the family room, breakfast nook, and kitchen. Halls are minimized downstairs and eliminated upstairs so you can enjoy the view as you move from room to room.

4 **Volumetrics**

▼ A feeling of spaciousness starts outside the front door with the copper-clad, barrel-vaulted entry. Inside, a vaulted ceiling soars from the foyer into the wide-open spaces of the family room. The curved theme of the exterior reappears inside in walls, ceilings, and windows.

2 **Entry excitement**

▶ Jack turned the hall closet around in order to create an attractive display wall that faces the front door.

3 **Through-views**

A glance in every direction provides a view into another room through enlarged doorways or open spaces.

CHANGE OF HEART

Families seldom use a formal area today, so the living room has become a small, concentrated getaway space.

The family room (*right*) is the heart of this home plan. When both spouses are through with their jobs,

The living room has become a small, concentrated getaway space. The family room (*right*) is the heart of this home plan.

the family gets together there, in the kitchen, and in the everyday sort of dining/breakfast room. These are the areas where they entertain their friends, too.

INDOOR/OUTDOOR TIES

People are also much more oriented to the out-of-doors, so the outdoors shouldn't be ignored in a home design. I think we're doing a much better job these days of using the land so that outdoor living becomes a more important part of the housing product. Landscaping is not just a box, and then you plant some shrubs. It's a coordinated design of land and housing concept.

In this house, we used a lot of corner windows to take advantage of the panoramic views of the wooded setting. The family room, kitchen, and master suite have French or sliding doors that access the back courtyard and deck.

7 Indoor/outdoor orientation   **5** Zoning

▲ Between meals, this is a popular spot! Kids will tackle their homework here, then scoot out the deck door for playtime. Later, Mom and Dad can sip coffee and quietly review the day.

8 Strategic storage   **10** Lots of light

▲ Kitchen patrol is a pleasure in a room well stocked with storage, the latest in appliances, and counter space. Recessed lighting and a stretch of windows brighten the work centers.

4 Volumetrics
8 Storage

▼ The true heart of the home, the family room draws everyone into its warm embrace with a crackling fire and a see-through to the kitchen. Open the peninsula doors and watch TV. Or, snuggle down with good company or a new novel, and enjoy the view, too.

SUITE RETREAT

We're seeing more and more of today's homeowners demanding a master bedroom suite that has closets to house all their casual, go-to-work, and sports-related clothes. That's because everything is so specialized these days.

Couples who regularly get up together and get dressed to go to work need a place that fits both of them comfortably. And they really require a spacious master bedroom suite to enjoy their health and fitness routines, as well. But they want their master suite to be both functional and fashionable at the same time.

Today's master suite must be functional and fashionable.

MAIN FLOOR LOCALE

Not everyone desires a two-story with the master suite up. We intentionally placed this suite (*right*) on the first floor, because today's homeowners want guests to see it, and they make sure they see it. They're very proud of it and love to show it off.

The master suite on the first floor works just as well for young parents as it does for an older couple. Parents like the separation from the children in the upstairs bedrooms. Should the older couple have overnight or weekend guests, the upstairs bedrooms also create more privacy for everyone.

④ Volumetrics   ⑩ Lots of light

▲ Cool teal and silver-gray tile, a barrel-vaulted ceiling, Hollywood lights, and dramatic cove lighting set a luxurious stage for bathing, shaving, and dressing in the master bathroom.

⑨ Architectural detailing   ⑩ Lots of light

▲ A three-course glass block treatment provides bonus lighting and private outdoor views. Separate shower and tub give you two ways to prepare for the day: a quick spruce-up or a leisurely pampering.

6 Master suite excitement

▲ The spacious master suite offers an oasis of quiet and relaxation in the midst of a bustling household. A private courtyard adds a touch of romance—and a separate exit to steal away for an early-morning run.

A ONE-TIME EXPENSE

Most of today's buyers have specific needs and

Architectural detailing is a one-time expense. It doesn't cost that much more to do it well.

wants in mind when they consider their dream home. Most don't move until they find a house that says, "This is the real me." It has to have most of the things they want right when they buy it. And they're willing to spend a little more on quality.

More houses have nice finishes now, and the style of the outside carries all the way through. I see a lot more attention to trim, ceiling treatments, and painting treatments (*above right*), because they're more affordable. The detail treatments costs less in proportion than does the increased price of the land, taxes, utilities, or maintenance. Architectural detailing is a one-time expense. It really doesn't cost that much more to do it well.

FOOTNOTES

Our featured Bloodgood house is 2,223 finished square feet and cost approximately $185,000 to build on a $54,000 lot (approximately $83 per square foot). The price did not include the landscaping design and interior wall coverings.

9 Architectural detailing **3** Through-views

▲ Corner windows and playful painted-on shutters and parapets turn a bare-bones box into a bright and cheery bedroom/play space any child would love.

10 Lots of light

▲ This charming mini-haven loft might have been an undereaves closet were it not for the vaulted ceiling jogging on up from the family room. From here you can keep tabs on everyone upstairs and down.

AFFORDABLE Style

BY
DENISE L. CARINGER
AND ROBERT E. DITTMER

Becky and Allen Jerdee with their children, Amy and Adam, and their cat.

Snappy update: a backdrop of white blinds and paint showcases crisp stripes and handmade accents. Topped with tile for casual family meals, the custom-made coffee table also corrals magazines.

"We're ordinary people who find beauty in ordinary things. The challenge? What can we put together today that will make us feel at home?"

Photographs: Scott Little
Design: Rebecca Jerdee

Once dim and dull, this '50s ranch has seen the light. Its bright new spirit reflects the work and ingenuity of Becky and Allen Jerdee—suburban "prospectors" who found treasure within their tract-house walls.

The Jerdees' home looks like its neighbors—until you walk inside.

Under green paint, heavy draperies, and dark carpet lay the treasure: simplicity. "It was a blank canvas on which we could do anything," says Becky.

An artist and craftsperson, Becky used paint and sponges to block-print a quilt on a home office wall. Typifying the family's high-style, low-cost ideas, the painted walls are something you can do, too.

FROM SUBURBAN TO SCANDINAVIAN

When the Jerdees traded their small-town Victorian for a suburban ranch, Becky admits, "I was depressed at first. I missed the character of the old house, and here we were in this *box*." Inspired by Scandinavian style— a blend of contemporary crispness with folkish charm—the family decid-ed to get back to basics. Out went the shag carpet and the dreary draperies, two elements that gobbled up not only space, but light. Next, they coated cel-ery-green walls with gallons of white paint, turning the living room into a luminous gathering spot. Instead of hanging artwork, Becky lettered the walls with soft-spoken messages.

Fresh and fun, the living room gets Scandinavian style from striped sofas upholstered by Becky and a tile-topped table she designed. Vertical blinds from JCPenney turn a trio of dated windows into a sleek modern accent, while homespun touches, like the country lawn chair, keep things cozy.

Restful pastels give depth to the wall and an aging chair.

"We missed the texture of our old Victorian house, so we tried to add some of that with antique architectural elements."

White paint enhances the details of country-crafted accessories. "I love the play of light on a series of white objects," Becky says.

AGING A RANCH WITH OLD-HOUSE ARTIFACTS

"After we moved our furniture in, we sat there and stared at this blank wall," Becky recalls. "We needed a focal point—a fireplace!" With one eye on style and the other on the checkbook, they faked a cozy illusion with an antique surround flanked by shelves—even a hearth.

Instead of a fire, artwork tinged with hot pinks and golds "blazes" in the fireplace opening. Above, homespun miniatures add nook-and-cranny appeal. Although fixed in place, a beautiful antique door, complete with a lace curtain, leads to daydreams of the past.

Teamwork: Allen's carpentry skills and Becky's designs get the job done.

"By creating our home together, we develop our skills and share a job well done. Wasn't it the poet Gibran who said, 'Work is love made visible'?"

For a country-modern look, Becky and Allen lavished white paint on the once-brown kitchen cabinets and removed some upper doors. Although contemporary, the striped wallpaper suggests old-fashioned wainscoting.

Even in antiques, the Jerdees choose to live with simple, functional objects.

FARMHOUSE FLAVOR FOR A '50s KITCHEN

Finding beauty in simple things, the Jerdees display white dishes, cookware, and handsome generic products on open kitchen shelves. To add character to the eating spot, Allen built shelves under the window, then nailed a chair rail to the adjoining wall.

With antique tile in mind, Becky decorated the kitchen walls with adhesive-backed paper that she cut into crisp tilelike patterns. A ceiling fan, an outdoor table and chairs—even a poster with an alfresco image—treat the family to porch-style charm no matter what the season.

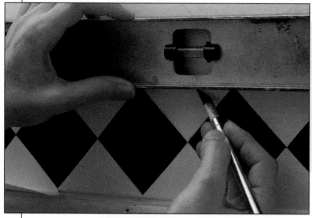

With a level and an artist's knife, Becky cuts adhesive-backed paper into "tiles."

"On a budget, we came up with more interesting and personal decorating ideas than if we'd been able to just go out and buy what we wanted."

Same layout, new look! To carry out the country-modern look, Allen softened the walls with mellow pine, then Becky stepped in with geometric designs cut from shelf paper. A new pedestal sink, mirror, and strip light finish the job.

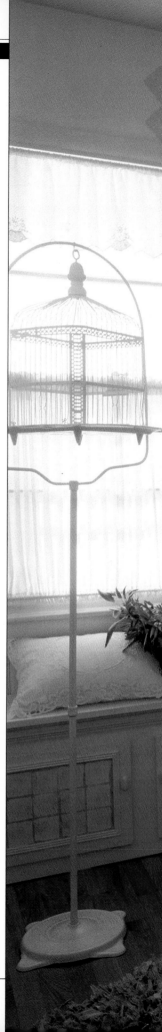

COUNTRY-INN CHARM FOR MODERN-DAY ROOMS

Peek inside the Jerdees' snug master bedroom, and it's hard to believe that this is a '50s tract house. Filmy curtains, eyelet, a window seat, antique quilts and countrified beadboard create a back-roads getaway smack in the center of suburbia. "We took the smallest bedroom," says Becky, "and Allen built the furniture. We put in what we thought were the elements of a great master suite but scaled them down." The headboard, for instance, nods to the massive beds favored by Victorians without overpowering the small space. Similarly, a grid of quilt-like squares painted on the wall adds country romance while preserving the airy white scheme. 🏠

The Jerdees have a knack for making rooms cozy and airy at the same time. After tossing the old draperies, the couple was pleasantly surprised at how light-filled their home could be. "The light changes from hour to hour," says Becky. "We use a lot of white to make the most of that."

MARK ROTHKO
WORKS ON PAPER

JUNE

SUMMER FUN

FAMILY STYLE

FUN, AFFORDABLE, BUILD-IT-YOURSELF
VACATION CABIN

BY TOM JACKSON

Vacation homes are not just for the rich,
*and this family proved it. They started with a tent, a plot of
land, and no construction experience. Two years and
$26,000 later they were fishing, gardening, and relaxing in
and around a handcrafted cabin of their own. Here's how.*

Mike Stull opens up for the weekend by unlocking the sturdy bifold security doors.

HOW THE CABIN GOT BUILT

Plenty of hard work preceded the carpentry. Trees were felled, the lot was graded, and a septic system was installed.

Bill and Nina Stull started their quest for a vacation home with a little cash and a lot of obstacles. They wanted a cabin that would sleep themselves and their two sons. They were both full-time schoolteachers. They had a very tight budget and no building experience.

After finding a secluded plot of land, however, they pitched their tents, put in a well, and went hunting for an architect who could translate their dreams into reality.

Architects J. Carson Bowler and John Cook developed a design that met the Stulls' needs with three strategies.

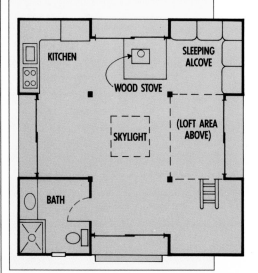

Floor plan labels: KITCHEN · SLEEPING ALCOVE · WOOD STOVE · SKYLIGHT · (LOFT AREA ABOVE) · BATH

"WHAT ACTUALLY CONVINCED ME TO DO THE PROJECT WAS THE STULLS' ENERGY AND SPIRIT."
—*Contractor Bruce Nachtigall*

The entry sign "MAMOTH WOODS" is short for "Mom and the men of the woods."

Bill experiments with drought- and deer-resistant plants. The planter is Nina's, created from driftwood and scraps.

Just big enough for weekend meals, the Stulls' 8 × 8-foot kitchen was designed to incorporate the antique hutch.

"WE WANTED IT OUTDOORSY— ALMOST A HIPPIE HAVEN."
— Nina Stull

HOW THE CABIN GOT BUILT

Erecting the shell of the cabin required the help of contractor Bruce Nachtigall. Working alongside the family, Bruce directed the framing and roofing, and provided guidance later for the finishing tasks.

First, the architects created a compact 24-foot-8-inch square design that makes efficient use of building materials.

Second, they made the design simple enough that the family could do much of the work.

And third, they introduced the Stulls to contractor Bruce Nachtigall who would guide them through the process.

"The Stulls and I hit it off great," says Nachtigall. "What actually convinced me to do the project was their energy and spirit. They were great people to work for." His advice for people who might want to tackle a simi-lar project: find a contractor you like and can communicate with.

After six weeks of work with Nachtigall, the Stulls had a shell they could finish themselves.

From that point on the family proceeded whenever time permitted, picking away at the many finishing tasks—building cabinets; installing paneling, trim, and flooring; laying carpet; and staining and sealing the wood surfaces—all on weekends and holidays. Many of the modular components were built in town during the week and hauled to the cabin site later.

Leisurely hours at the cabin leave plenty of time for reading and puttering, and a chance for Nina to crochet.

Mike uses an uprooted tree stump for an archery backdrop.

Raftable rivers were a primary consideration in the Stulls' choice of a building site.

THE BENEFITS OF RELAXATION Downtime and idle hours are important components of the Stulls' weekends at the cabin, and the rustic mosaic of knotty pine paneling provides the perfect ambience.

Stained-glass panels with a floral design by Nina bring natural light into the bath enclosure.

Tucked underneath the roof slope, a cozy 6 × 8-foot sleeping loft for the parents is accessible by ladder.

"THE CABIN IS FOR US. IT HAS MADE FOR A HAPPY MARRIAGE."
—Nina Stull

HOW THE CABIN GOT BUILT

After six weeks of labor-intensive carpentry, the Stulls had a roof overhead and shelter from the elements. From then on, the family tackled the finishing tasks on spare weekends and holidays.

Nina, who did a lot of the carpentry and cabinetry says, "We were very brave to even start it. All the work was done by handsaw and adrenaline."

The cabin has no interior walls save for the bathroom enclosure. Each corner of the cabin anchors an activity: cooking, bathing, and at the two banquettes, sitting and sleeping. Four sliding glass doors and a skylight bring in the sunshine.

Shiplap knotty pine covers the interiors. To ensure that the wood's rustic brown, blue, and tan patterns matched, Nachtigall spent a day sorting out the pieces at the lumberyard.

The kitchen measures a compact 8 × 8 feet and opens to the rest of the cabin. When Nina found an old Hoosier hutch at an antiques sale, she had the kitchen designed around it.

For sleeping, the parents have a 6 × 8-foot sleeping loft, tucked under the slope of the roof. The boys bed down on the banquette cushions.

A centrally located wood stove provides the cabin with heat and helps divide the banquette area from the kitchen.

When the Stulls aren't using the cabin, they lock it up with large bifold door panels they designed themselves.

The costs: $13,000 for the shell (including fees and electrical, plumbing, grading, and foundation work), $11,000 for the finishing (including stove, refrigerator, and shower), and $2,000 for the septic system.

Now that the cabin is finished and the boys are older, Nina and Bill use the cabin mainly as a parents' getaway. "The cabin is for us," says Nina. "It has made for a happy marriage. It's our retreat. We both lead busy lives all week and this is our chance to get away." BH&G

Day's end finds the family winding their way through the redwoods back to the city.

SEE THE LIGHT!
EASY AND ENJOYABLE GREENHOUSE ADD-ONS

Glassy greenhouse spaces bring the outdoors in. Or, is it the other way around? No matter. The result is a best-of-both-worlds room.

DARE TO DECORATE

Afraid you wouldn't know what to put in one of these gridded glass encasements? Do what these two owners did—simply take your cues from the great outdoors. Greenery, earthbound colors, and warm woods are the ties that bind interior landscapes to the close-at-hand outdoors in these homes.

A small greenhouse wall made a big difference in the third-floor St. Louis apartment (*right*). Formerly walled off from the outside world, the dining area became light filled and spacious with the addition. A forest of plants and a marble-topped table give the space a sunny, resort feeling even when snow dances on the glass panes.

In the Seattle dining area (*right below*), lush surroundings inspired the abundant floral fabric on the table and pillow-strewn seats. Swirling oak—on the floor, banquette, and vintage cabinet—creates a warm environment.

GREEN THUMBS NOT REQUIRED

Once reserved for commercial nurseries and avid horticulturists, an attached-to-the-house greenhouse is now looked upon as a way to gain more living space—and more light—without going to all the expense of building a new room addition. Available in kit form, these glass structures can simply be appended to a home's exterior.

The size and shape of an attached greenhouse depends on the number and kinds of components you order. Typically, small to medium-size enclosures cost $3,000 to $10,000 (excluding assembly). That's about two-thirds less than contractor-built additions.

To find out more about installing a greenhouse space in your home, look under "Greenhouse Builders" in the Yellow Pages or check for materials at a building supply store. 🏠

Even a modest greenhouse wall enlarges interior spaces—physically and visually.

Lots of glass, warm woods, and blooming fabrics make every meal a picnic.

JULY

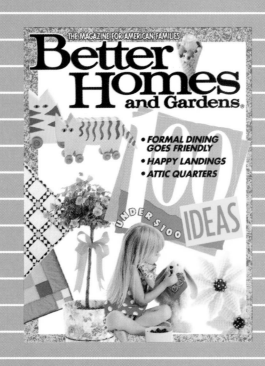

FORMAL DINING GOES FRIENDLY
GRACIOUS EATING IN A RELAXED SETTING

By Michael Walsh

This room is inviting whether the menu calls for tuna salad or salad niçoise.

Here's proof that a separate, formal dining room can also be a friendly one. Speaking with a country French accent, this room doesn't distinguish between family meals and big-deal dinner parties.

Informal furnishings

A dining room's graciousness need not come from such fragile trappings as twinkling crystal overhead or polished mahogany. For a more approachable atmosphere, replace the formal with more relaxed—but equally honest and beautiful—materials such as honey-hued oak and mellow pine. More stately than snooty, an oak armoire doubles as a china cabinet in this dining room. The oak settee offers two more seats when the dining table is fully extended. A pine Welsh cupboard displays collectibles and furthers the woody warmth.

As practical as it is pretty, this stripped-pine Welsh cupboard is a clever cache for cutlery and linens.

Fresh fabrics

Use coordinating wallpaper and fabric generously to promote a friendly atmosphere and to pull a room's look together. Here, tied-on seat cushions add comfort to simple, ladder-back chairs, and link the seats to the settee and valance. The fabric wears the same pattern as the wallpaper, which warmly wraps the room just above a white chair rail. A compatible fabric pulls the window seat's cushion and the chandelier's shades into the mix of materials. Pillows and gingham table linens lend more subtle, country-style pattern.

The final step

Sometimes what you leave out can be as important as what you put in. Here, the absence of an area rug under the table shows just how inevitably elegant a polished wood floor can be.

HAPPY LANDINGS
ZONE THEM FOR STYLE

Your stairway landing may offer only a small slice of space, but it could be just the right portion for a snug—and handy—retreat. Here's a sampling of ways you can carve out an inviting nook.

Pillow talk

A built-in window seat and an artfully arranged collection of plump pillows are the simple ingredients for a stylish, only-steps-away getaway (*right*). Brightened by the purposely undressed window and sunny yellow fabric, this little hot spot practically insists that passersby take time out to read, daydream, or simply enjoy a well-deserved breather.

This handy hangout offers a bonus as well: The banquette's top flips up to reveal stashing space for blankets, sweaters, and the like.

Located on the way to the third-floor attic, this stylish rest stop beckons with cozy cushions.

Comfort zone

Create a cozy cranny from an often-overlooked space—the connecting platform for two flights of stairs (*below left*). An ideal spot from which to rise above the tensions of the day, this en route rest stop is wired for twilight reading and softened with cozy pillows and a cuddle-up quilt. This banquette also holds a storage reserve, making the spot as practical as it is pretty.

Show your stuff

A stair landing can be a wonderful stage upon which to spotlight your style (*below right*). Located between kitchen and living room, this landing's gear is gathered from the brass, chinese blue ware, and other antiques collections found in the rest of the house. Greenery warms up the grouping.

PHOTOGRAPH: JOHN VAUGHAN. DESIGN: AGNES BOURNE, ASID. FIELD EDITOR: BARBARA EAST CATHCART

Adding two wall lamps makes this landing a handy getaway, perfect for twilight reading.

PHOTOGRAPH: JESSIE WALKER ASSOCIATES. DESIGN: SUSAN KROEGER, LTD.

This stair landing becomes center stage for a cast of collectibles, gathered in a dramatic vignette.

PHOTOGRAPH: LAURIE BLACK AND ROSLYN BANISH / ARX

DESIGN: SHARON CAMPBELL. FIELD EDITOR: HELEN HEITKAMP

ATTIC QUARTERS
CREATE A PINT-SIZE PENTHOUSE

STRATEGY ONE: Raise the ceiling for a spacious feeing.

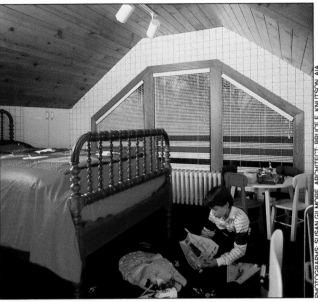

STRATEGY THREE: Add bright colors to lighten the room.

Rambling attics can be perfect kids' retreats: They're roomy, private, and full of the kind of nooks and crannies kids love. Here is a child-pleasing remodel complete with several smart conversion strategies that will work under the rafters of most any attic.

STRATEGY ONE:
Raise the ceiling

Once merely storage space, this attic now buzzes with activity as the living quarters for 5- and 8-year-old brothers. To bring the rooms to life, the owners had to overcome some typical attic obstacles: in this case, inadequate headroom, a massive chimney, and a protruding heat stack.

For better ceiling height, they raised the attic's collar ties by nearly a foot. (Collar ties are the overhead beams that run across the attic from one sloped wall to the other at or above the ceiling.) Now, the ceiling measures 8 feet at its tallest point—a height that should be comfortable even when the boys are grown.

Special note: Unless they're just for show, collar ties serve as functional elements that keep the roof from pushing

STRATEGY TWO: A skylight in the ceiling splashes light into the bath.

apart the walls, so consult with an architect or engineer if you're considering moving or removing them.

The family boxed in the heating stack and chimney to make them as inconspicuous as possible. Spongy acoustical tile turned the chimney into a freestanding bulletin board.

STRATEGY TWO:
Bring in light

Although the original attic was blessed with large windows, partitioning the space into rooms blocked the

free flow of light. The solution: supplement the lighting from overhead. In the south-facing bedroom, track lights proved adequate to complete the lighting plan. In the daytime the room remains sunny. In the bath, a new skylight, operable to provide both sunshine and ventilation, solves the problem of a too-dark space. The family also added a skylight to the north-facing bedroom, to boost the softer light there.

STRATEGY THREE:
Color it bright

White backgrounds and eye-popping accents are guaranteed kid pleasers. In the older boy's room (*above right*), primary colors stripe mini-blinds, which were custom-fit to the slanted windows. In his brother's room (*above left*), stripes take to the floor on a small area rug; the underlying wood floors provide a hard, smooth surface for rolling toy trucks or building block towers.

Primary colors continue in the shared bath, coordinating with the effect achieved in the bedrooms. In the tub and on the floor, vibrant-blue accent tiles play off a field of white. All three attic rooms wear wood-strip ceilings for a touch of natural warmth.

AUGUST

THE MAGAZINE FOR AMERICAN FAMILIES

Better Homes and Gardens

- COTTAGE CHARM
- 3 EAT-IN KITCHENS
- SEW-EASY DECORATING
- FIX A FIXER-UPPER
- GOOD MORNING!

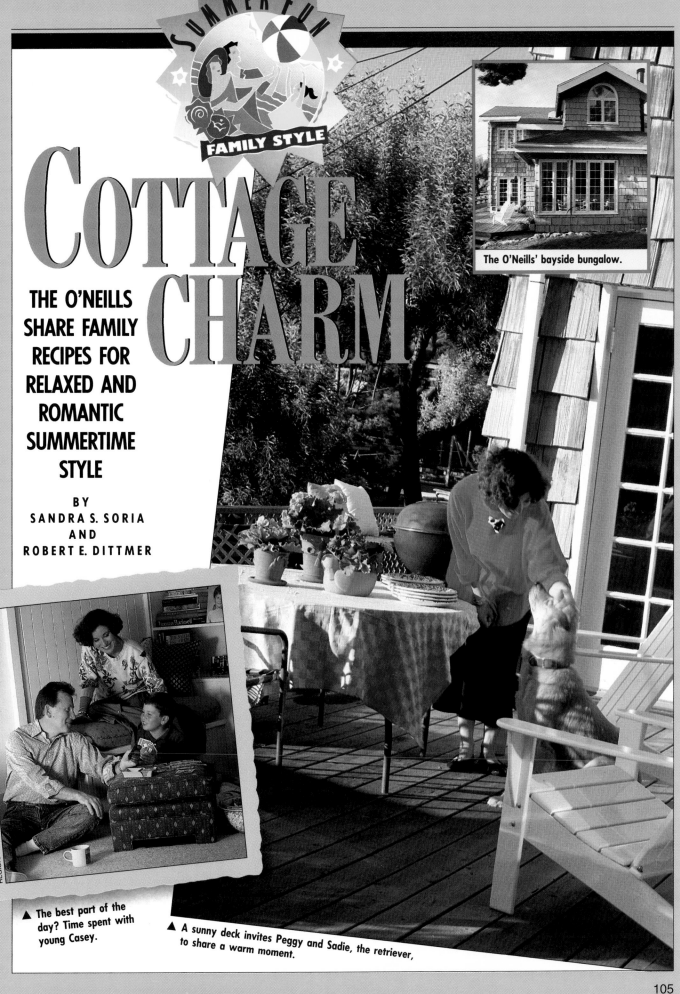

COTTAGE CHARM

THE O'NEILLS SHARE FAMILY RECIPES FOR RELAXED AND ROMANTIC SUMMERTIME STYLE

BY
SANDRA S. SORIA
AND
ROBERT E. DITTMER

The O'Neills' bayside bungalow.

PHOTOGRAPHS: LAURIE BLACK
REGIONAL EDITOR: HELEN HEITKAMP

▲ The best part of the day? Time spent with young Casey.

▲ A sunny deck invites Peggy and Sadie, the retriever, to share a warm moment.

▲ Creamy hues and see-through wicker lighten the home.

For Tom, Peggy, and Casey O'Neill, this home is truly where their hearts are. Brimming with sunlight and friendly furnishings, the house embraces like a warm hug.

The lure of warmth and a longtime respect for the sea led Minnesota-born Tom and Massachusetts native Peggy to San Francisco, where they met some 20 years ago. But it was more like love at first sight—and maybe even the hand of fate—that drew them to the 1896 cottage, perched a stone's throw from the bay.

"WE WON'T PUT ANYTHING IN OUR HOME THAT CASEY CAN'T JUMP ON, BECAUSE LITTLE BOYS HAVE TO JUMP."

—Peggy

The couple was happily settled in a Victorian home in the city, when Peggy ran across an ad for the bayside dwelling in the Sunday paper. "We had no intention of moving," Tom recalls, "but when Peggy read that ad to me, something moved me to drive here the next day. I brought her back the same night, and we were moved in before we knew what hit us."

To history-major Tom, a fascination with the home's origins—it was built by a treasure-smuggling sea captain—sparked the love affair. The dwelling's colorful character also charmed Peggy, and she remained true to that when decorating. Easygoing wicker and whitewashed woods nod to the cottage-by-the-sea personality. Then, durable fabrics and warmer-than-wood carpet meet present-day needs.

◄ Cookie crumbs and tennis shoes aren't out of bounds in this living room with a view.

▼ Humble pine "relaxes" the formal dining room.

Two-career crunch

For the O'Neills, there's no place like a relaxed home—and it's easy to see why. Peggy often starts her day at 5 a.m., when she scours the city flower market for blooms to sell in her two local flower shops. As vice president of sales for a construction firm, Tom regularly logs 12-hour days. They also share the duties of raising 9-year-old Casey, whose schedule includes computer class, soccer, and little league ("I like to keep busy," reports Casey). After a high-speed day, home is a place to downshift to a slower pace.

Family ties

Cozy spaces and put-your-feet-up furnishings keep the family at ease. "I think you have to use things in your home that make you feel good," says Peggy. In the master bedroom, wicker,

> ## "I DRIVE HOME EACH NIGHT WITH REAL ANTICIPA-TION OF GETTING BACK HERE."
>
> **—Tom**

blossoms, and softened sunlight spell tranquillity.

After spinning off in separate directions on weekdays, the O'Neill trio prefers to share evening and weekend hours. "Sometimes when the phone rings," Peggy admits, "I stand in the background and shake my head. Family times are that precious."

To make daily family reunions special, Peggy, Tom, and Casey celebrate even ordinary activities. For example, each evening meal is an event to savor.

Peggy often rises before the sun does to head to the flower market, so Tom gets Casey revved up for the day. A remodeled bathroom makes room enough for two.

▲ A clothespin giraffe grips the recipe for Casey's specialty. "He loves to make chocolate chip cookies," says Peggy, "mostly so he can eat the dough."

"When Peggy works on Saturday, it's Casey's and my day," says Tom, ▶ whose roles include little league and soccer coach as well as father.

▲ The O'Neills' style is easy to duplicate. The secret? Keep it casual.

▲ In the master bedroom, a mix of fine-lined wicker, delicate flowers, and sherbet shades pleases the eye and soothes the soul. Tailored shutters match the room's simple elegance and diffuse harsh sunlight to further soften the setting.

"WE TEND
TO BE
SPONTANEOUS
WHEN WE
ENTERTAIN;
THAT
WAY EVERYONE
RELAXES."
—Tom

COTTAGE CHARM

The O'Neills host thrown-together gatherings with close friends rather than orchestrate big-deal dinner parties. ▶

▼ Potted flowers, a checkered tablecloth, and sturdy dinnerware promote a picnic atmosphere. Friends fall into the fun-under-the-sun feeling.

▶ After a hectic, suit-and-tie week, Tom loosens up with jeans and a few friends.

"Dinner is relaxed but there's a ritual about it," says Tom. "We all help put it together—and we almost always have candles. It's Casey's job to light them."

Peggy and Tom added a double-duty eating area and family room off the kitchen to make space for the family affairs. A hearth of stones found on their property makes a heartwarming focal point. Countrified furnishings and accents, such as a herd of cow collectibles, add down-home charm.

Entertaining ideas

French doors lead the way from cozy eating area to great outdoors—where the O'Neills entertain. A typical gathering means a few pals and casual cuisine, served on the deck. "Tom usually grills a salmon and I put together a pasta salad," says Peggy. "You can't get much simpler than that."

111

3 EAT-IN KITCHENS

BY WILLIAM L. NOLAN

Tacos and chips in the dining room? If that's the only place you can get a table at your house, use one of these space-stretchers to gain a kitchen eating area.

- **REWORK THE PLAN** by shifting walls, doors, and windows, and rearranging the built-ins.
- **BUMP OUT A WALL** to gain a few extra feet for a table and chairs near the work area.
- **ANNEX ADJOINING SPACE** that has outlived its original purpose and no longer earns its keep.

▲ The microwave is tucked under the island countertop, handy for snacks when the kids do homework at the table.

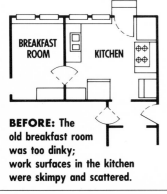

BREAKFAST ROOM   KITCHEN

BEFORE: The old breakfast room was too dinky; work surfaces in the kitchen were skimpy and scattered.

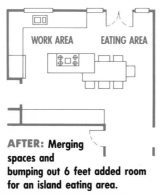

WORK AREA   EATING AREA

AFTER: Merging spaces and bumping out 6 feet added room for an island eating area.

ISLAND OASIS

Savvy stretching nets a sit-down island

1 Lots of light, loads of work space, and an eating area big enough to seat the whole family—these were the must-haves that shaped this kitchen revamp in Atlanta. To fill the bill, architect Norman Askins bumped out the rear wall a few feet and merged the old kitchen, service hall, and cubby-hole breakfast room into one big space.

SPLIT-LEVEL ISLAND

The new plan centers on a two-level island that seats six. Dropping the countertop a few inches at one end segregated work and eating space and yielded table-height dining. Big windows and French doors make the room light and airy.

ARCHITECT: NORMAN ASKINS. INTERIOR DESIGN: KATHY GUYTON. KITCHEN DESIGN: JOHN FARILL, HOUSE OF DENMARK. PHOTOGRAPHS: MIKE MORELAND. REGIONAL EDITOR: RUTH L. REITER

Minus a few interior walls, this revamped kitchen gained space for an island work center/eating area that seats six. The tabletop is cantilevered for extra legroom.

BUNGALOW BUMP-OUT

A few more feet made a world of difference

2 Three feet here, 6 feet there—that's all it took to ease the space crunch in Tom and Kathy Munro's kitchen. The Munros bumped out one wall of their Seattle bungalow 6 feet to grab room for a sun-drenched eating area and easier access to the garden. Pushing out the adjoining wall 3 feet yielded lateral stretch in the work area.

PERFECT MATCH

Period proportions and detailing fuse the bump-out with the main structure, enhancing the home's 1920s bungalow character. The new roof pitch, fascia, and window trim match that of the old, and deep overhangs repeat those on the original house. Window shapes and sizes—purposely mixed—follow a trait characteristic of bungalows of this vintage. Inside, moldings on the cabinet fronts echo the square-pane window grids.

▲ It's just a step from the table to the terrace! The bump-out's walls flare at the bottom like those on the original house.

▼ Built-ins in the work area extend past the island, putting extra storage and work space within arm's reach of the table.

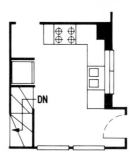

BEFORE: Skimpy square footage forced the family to eat in the dining room.

AFTER: With a 6-foot bump-out at one end and a 3-footer along the side, the room measures up.

French doors and sidelights in this bump-out eating area put the garden on view at tableside. Vaulting the bump-out all the way to the peak heightened its roomy look.

DESIGN: PATRICIA BRENNAN. PHOTOGRAPHS: MIKE JENSEN. REGIONAL EDITOR: TRISH MAHARAM

CORNER BANQUETTE

Table space was hiding in the laundry and a closet

3 Four children and dual careers were creating rush-hour gridlock in Janet and Bob Mincer's 60-year-old San Diego kitchen. Traffic bottlenecked in the cramped 9×11-foot space—the only doorway led to the dining room—and there wasn't even enough room for a snack bar. Fortunately, bonus space lay close at hand: the adjoining laundry room and entry closet. Annexing these areas gave the Mincers a comfy banquette dining nook plus a handy new doorway that links the kitchen to the front entry.

ARCHITECT: TARASUCK, FOLEY, AND ASSOCIATES. REGIONAL EDITOR: SHARON HAVEN. PHOTOGRAPHS: KIM BRUN

BEFORE: Cramped quarters in the kitchen left no room for a table; traffic to the patio tracked through the work area.

AFTER: The old laundry made way for a dining nook; a new door routes traffic through the entry foyer.

▲ **Big windows** opposite the table catch the morning sun and tie the kitchen to the patio. A door in the alcove beyond provides new access from the front hall to the kitchen.

A space-saving ▶ corner banquette lines the Mincers' new dining nook. Revamped built-ins in the work area terminate in a handy peninsula serving bar near the table.

DESIGNS FOR BUTTERICK

Better Homes and Gardens®

BY DENISE L. CARINGER
AND ROBERT E. DITTMER

SEW–EASY DECORATING

A LITTLE ROMANCE

Crisp white fabric stitched into romantic bed linens and curtains can turn a mere bedroom into a great retreat. Soft and soothing, this suite scheme starts with patterns available from your fabric store and ends with your own personal touches.

Create a "family reunion" on a bedside table. These no-sew, fabric-wrapped frames make it easy to surround your loved ones with softness.

F

abrics edged with ruffles and ribbon make it "sew" simple to thread a little romance into your life. Look for this frilly yardage at major fabric stores.

NOSTALGIC PILLOWS
Settle back on a pile of squashy pillows. The ruffled neck roll and shams (for both standard and "European square" pillows) are a snap to craft, thanks to fabrics that come with the frills built in.

SCALLOPED CURTAIN
With a little stitchery, you can give any room an old-fashioned point of view. Our scalloped curtain, topped with a snappy bias-striped valance, joins with a comfy chair to create a mellow time-out spot.

PATTERN FOR SUCCESS
Inviting, isn't it? A pillow-plumped bed and serene pastels bid welcome after a hectic day.

The Van Allens.

FIX A FIXER-UPPER

This teacher camped out for eight days to buy a row house for $200.

> "**A**t the time, I was single and making $17,000 a year. The only way I was ever going to get a house was by homesteading."
>
> —Catherine Clack Van Allen

ALL ABOARD THE REHAB EXPRESS

In August of '82, the prospects of home ownership were not very bright for Catherine, an inner-city schoolteacher. When a Baltimore urban renewal program dangled 348 ramshackle fixer-uppers for $200 plus closing costs, house-hungry Catherine bit.

TRUE GRIT

The $200 "bargain" contract required her to bring the 1855 trash-littered row house to code by August of 1984. Bowed front and back walls and a badly leaking roof were just two of many problems that Catherine faced.

She immediately hired workers to help her clean up and stabilize the most precarious sections of the building. Then she developed plans for each floor and went back to city officials to find financial assistance.

◀ **BUILT IN 1855,** Catherine's delapidated row house had been an abandoned Chinese laundry for more than 10 years.

▲ **AFTER THE RENOVATION,** Catherine married Peter Van Allen, and her family grew to include stepson Peter, Jr., 15, (top photo, left) and baby Nicholas.

◀ **CATHERINE HIRED** a sign company's crane to lift a $150 spiral staircase "find" into place just before the front wall was finished.

▼ **SHE LEARNED** to mortar as she worked her way around the crumbling building.

Because the century-plus-old house was situated within a historical district, she landed a 30-year, $40,000 loan at 7½-percent interest from a state agency for restoring the building.

For the next 20 months, an inexperienced Catherine got a hands-on education—with the help of two friends—on the finer points of construction.

Three months before her rehab deadline, she hired a contractor ("the smartest thing I did") to finish the project. To finance this, she borrowed $10,000 from her mother and an additional $14,000 from a Baltimore historic and architectural preservation program. In September 1984, she moved in. 🏠

WHAT SHE PAID

Monthly mortgage payment: $520.99. Financing: $40,000, 30-year loan at 7½ percent from a state housing rehabilitation program; $14,000 loan from a city historic and architectural preservation program.

A $10,000 loan from her mother brought total expenditure of renovating the house to $64,000.

WHAT SHE GOT

● Three-story row house, 14 feet wide by 45 feet deep
● Two bedrooms, one bath
● 1½-story efficiency apartment (later private quarters for teenaged stepson)

▲ **HOME SWEET HOME** with bargains from Goodwill and "alleys."

▼ **MOM PROVIDED** the kitchen tile. The antique stove cost $200.

PHOTOGRAPHS: MAXWELL MACKENZIE. ARCHITECT/DESIGNER: CATHERINE CLACK VAN ALLEN. REGIONAL EDITOR: EILEEN A. DEYMIER

PHOTOGRAPHS: JOAN VANDERSCHUIT. DESIGN: DICK FORD. REGIONAL EDITOR: SHARON HAVEN. ILLUSTRATION: MIKE HENRY

GO-O-O-D MORNING!
GREET THE DAY WITH A HIS-AND-HER BATH

BY JAMES A.
HUFNAGEL

Tired of waking up to a wait for the bathroom? Pamper yourselves with a winning bath-dressing room combination like this, and the two of you can get ready for work as quickly as one.

SOLO OR DUET

With twin sinks, double walk-in closets, abundant counter space, a compartmented toilet, a sit-down cosmetics center, and plenty of floor space, you needn't wor-

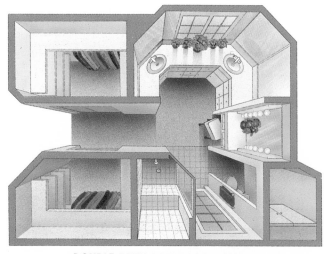

DOUBLE-DUTY BATHROOM LAYOUT
Start with twin dressing rooms, add two sinks, a quick-splash shower, and a make-up vanity, and you have a get-up-and-go bath.

▲ White cabinets and white tile brighten the lavatory bay. Double sinks give the homeowners space to rise and shine without bumping elbows.

ry about getting in each other's way when time comes for the morning rush hour. The closets serve as a sound buffer between the bath and the adjacent bedroom, so one spouse can catch a few extra winks, even if the other wants to sing in the spacious shower. In the bathroom, corner medicine cabinets and angled basins, set into a

122

Wall-size mirrors here and in the lavatory area amplify artificial and natural light. Multiple reflections also magnify the sense of space.

◀ **Crowned with a round-top window, the makeup center's mirror reflects the dressing area.**

◀ **The pattern of the arch over the entry to the bath is playfully repeated in the window over the makeup mirror.**

U-shaped vanity, flank a pair of casement windows. One corner accommodates a 3½ × 5-foot shower. A private closet for the toilet tucks into another corner. Between the shower and closet, a French door opens to a sheltered balcony.

CAPTURING FIRST LIGHT

The owners are early risers, so the design makes the most of natural light. Besides the casement windows over the vanity, a 5×7-foot skylight boosts brightness over the dressing area. A fan-shaped clerestory window that was custom-made to match existing windows on the front of the house tops the cosmetics center.

The bath gleams *before* dawn, too, thanks to re-

◀ **An angled shower enclosure leads the floor plan out to an enclosed deck. The tucked-away toilet adds privacy.**

Louvered ▶ bypass doors improve air circulation in the dressing area's spacious, well-organized closets.

cessed downlights in the soffits over the vanity and theatrical fixtures on each side of the cosmetic center. Wall-size mirrors here and in the lavatory area amplify both artificial and natural light. Their multiple reflections also magnify the sense of space. ▨

SEPTEMBER

THE MAGAZINE FOR AMERICAN FAMILIES

Better Homes
and Gardens

- COUNTRY-STYLE KIDS' ROOM
- THE NEW FAMILY ROOM
- MULTI-COOK KITCHEN

COUNTRY STYLE KID'S ROOM
VINTAGE FURNISHINGS IN A YOUTHFUL SCHEME
By Pamela C. Wilson

PHOTOGRAPHS: LAURIE BLACK AND ROSLYN BANISH/ARX. DESIGN: SUSAN M. ERICKSON. FIELD EDITOR: HELEN HEITKAMP

Unpretentious rustic antiques are charming—and practical—choices for a child's room.

Should antiques be off-limits in children's rooms? Not necessarily. Many old pieces are exceptionally sturdy and, as you'll see here, right at home in youthful settings.

Everything old is used again

Many antiques lovers believe that the way to truly enjoy their vintage treasures is to *use* them, not just admire them from afar. A believer herself, Susan Erickson has furnished her 5-year-old son Cole's room with assorted pieces from America's past. Here are the elements at play.

● **A youth bed** holds center stage. This decades-old, handcrafted beauty is the perfect fit—for the small room and for young Cole. To facilitate quiet-time play, Susan and her husband, Mark, fashioned a plywood shelf to fit across

Bedtime bonus: a painted shelf provides a flat surface for play. The shelf is easily removed and stowed.

the foot of the pint-size bed. When not in use for building castles and other imaginary structures, the painted shelf can be easily stored in a closet.

● **A corner cupboard**—recently fitted with shelves—makes a handsome and handy storage unit for Cole's books and play gear. Susan acquired the rustic antique cupboard in trade for one of her vintage quilts.

● **A library table** provides a display surface for Cole's favorite playthings. As the child's interests change over the years, so too will the table's role—it can become a homework station.

● **Assorted wicker baskets** offer additional storage for toys to keep ever-creeping clutter under wraps.

● **A pinstriped wall covering and miniblinds** are tailored to the room's simple style. 🄱🄷🄶

125

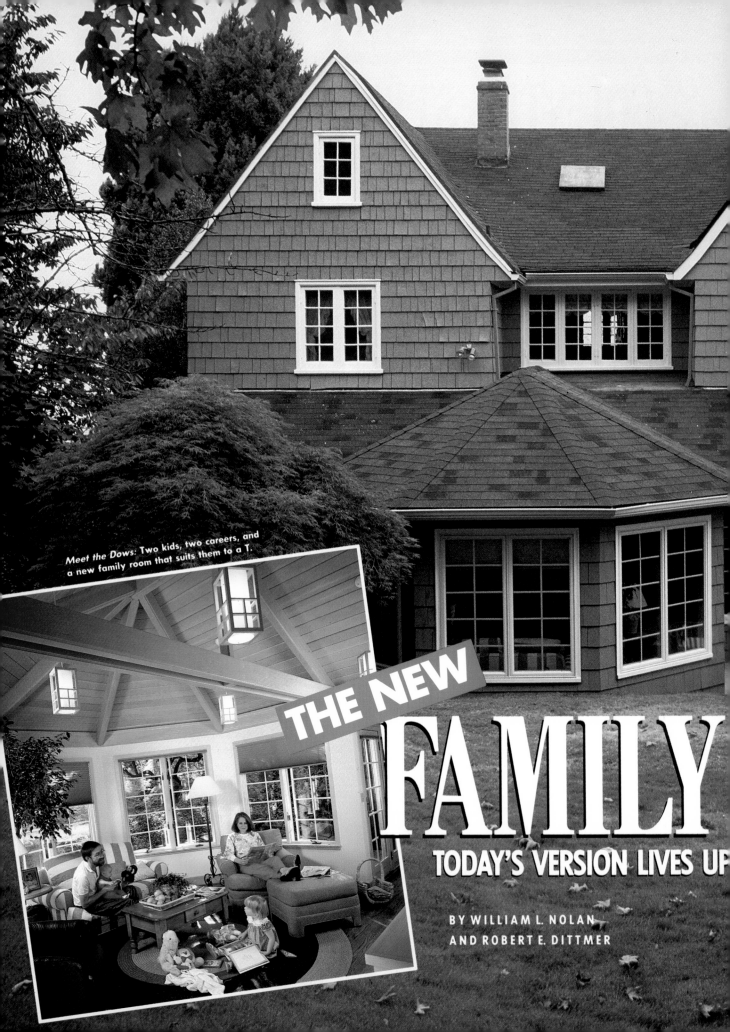

Meet the Dows: Two kids, two careers, and a new family room that suits them to a T.

THE NEW

FAMILY

TODAY'S VERSION LIVES UP

BY WILLIAM L. NOLAN
AND ROBERT E. DITTMER

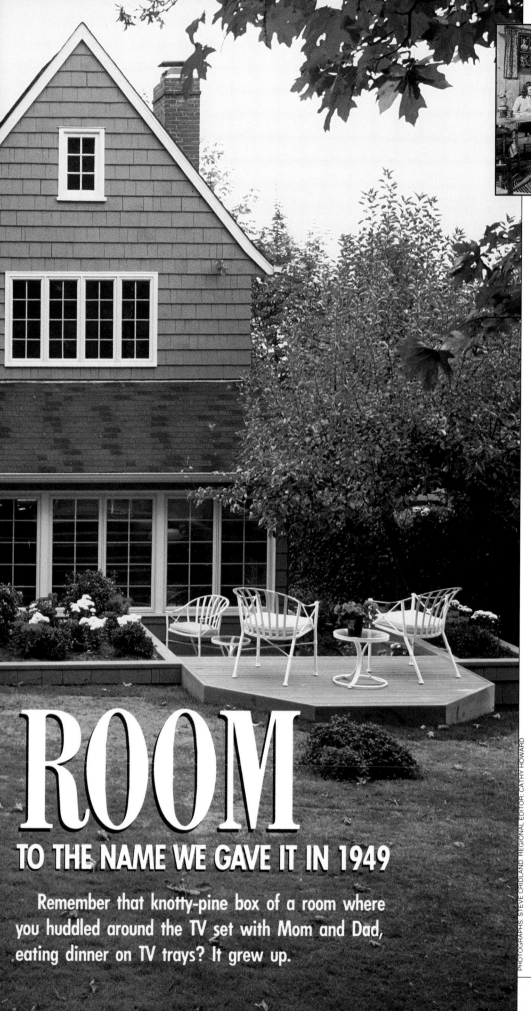

▲ 1940s

Cozy but closed in. Family rooms used to be dinky dens furnished with hand-me-downs from the living room.

◀ 1990s

Bye-bye, box. Today's window-lined family room yields added space, extra light, expansive views.

. . . .

MORE COMFORTS, NEW CONVENIENCE

- Room for games, TV, romps with the kids
- Outdoor living area
- Seamless blend of new and old
- Easygoing, hard-wearing furnishings
- Clever lighting
- Quiet corners for working at home
- Media built-ins
- Built-in wet bar
- Abundant storage

. . . .

A second child on the way prompted Russell and Alexis Dow to take a hard look at their 1920s two-story. The verdict: cramped quarters for an active family of four.

Sound familiar? We thought so, too, so we asked the Dows to help us fete the 40th birthday of the family room, which our building editors named exactly 40 years ago this month. Working with architect John

ROOM
TO THE NAME WE GAVE IT IN 1949

Remember that knotty-pine box of a room where you huddled around the TV set with Mom and Dad, eating dinner on TV trays? It grew up.

◀ **BEFORE:**
The Dows' vintage two-story lacked space for family activities—indoors and out. The rear wall isolated the backyard; a single door opened from the kitchen, and the rear elevation looked unbalanced.

DAVID PAPAZIAN

◀ **DURING:**
The add-on takes shape: new family spaces downstairs, a finish-later bath upstairs. The new bath wing balances the original rear gable. The addition was sheathed with plywood and cedar shake siding.

KARLIS GRANTS

◀ **AFTER:**
Savvy design fuses old and new. The old attic window moved into the new gable; four new windows below match others on the second floor. French doors and a two-level deck mate the house with the lawn.

STEVE CRIDLAND

ARCHITECT: GILBERT/HASENBERG ARCHITECTS. INTERIOR DESIGN: ROBERT E. DITTMER. CONTRACTOR: NEIL KELLY COMPANY, DESIGNERS/REMODELERS

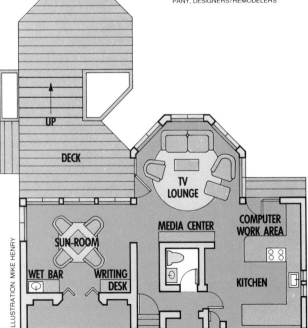

ILLUSTRATION: MIKE HENRY

UP

DECK

SUN-ROOM

WET BAR

WRITING DESK

TV LOUNGE

MEDIA CENTER

COMPUTER WORK AREA

KITCHEN

Flexibility keys the plan to 1990s lifestyles. Work and play spaces adjoin the kitchen; sliding doors turn one room into two.

Hasenberg and the Western Wood Products Association, the Dows gained a state-of-the-art family retreat that could put *your* house in tune with the '90s, too!

THREE ROOMS IN ONE

Hasenberg came up with a 3-in-1 room addition: a TV lounge, a sun-room sitting area, and a home work center. The sun-room adjoins the living room and links it to the garden. Bifold glass doors replaced the original living room window. They're flanked by handy built-ins crafted from Douglas fir: a wet bar with wine cooler below, stemware storage above; a desk with file drawers below, glass-front bookshelves above. A sliding door

> "*We didn't want to move. We like the neighborhood.*"
> —**Alexis Dow**

closes off the TV lounge from the sun-room when guests arrive before the kids turn in.

The garden room bridges the gap between interior and exterior spaces with its sleek and sunny style. Airy rattan furnishings establish a relaxing, resortlike mood. Set up for casual conversation, the seating pieces encircle a ready-to-serve coffee table. Underfoot, a soft area rug anchors the grouping.

All done, and it's ▶
gorgeous! The Dows toast
their new sun-room with
friends Anne and John
Mercer.

▲ Big, sunny windows by Andersen overlook the deck and the lawn.
At the panes, Verosol pleated shades diffuse strong sunlight to a
golden glow, or pull up and out of the way. The patio-perfect
rattan pieces help to blur the distinction between indoors and out.

Bring the garden in! Today's family spaces annex the great outdoors. Here, big windows flank strategically placed French doors.

▲ Home entertainment, 1990s-style: Stylish built-ins stow audio and video gear.

MEDIA CABINETMAKER: TAMARA BOYD, THE WOOD WORKSHOP

"I like the practical flow— especially the transition between outdoors and in."

—Russell Dow

▲ Outfit your family spaces for the '90s with built-ins tailored for high-tech hardware. The Dows house their gear in a nook near the kitchen. Alexis gets input from daughter Kaitlin.

French doors and big windows open the new spaces to the deck and lawn. Handy to the sun-room, the TV lounge, and the service hall, the doors lure family and guests onto the deck.

In the lounging area, hefty trusses of Douglas fir span the windowed bay under a vaulted ceiling; fir paneling warms the sloped areas.

CUSTOM STORAGE

Abundant, well-planned storage helps our 1990s family room handle household hubbub while maintaining a sleek, stylish composure. The TV lounge features an elegantly symmetrical media wall. Double doors hide the TV screen when it's not in use; metal fins inside the drawers keep tapes and albums organized. Woodcrafter Tamara Boyd built the media wall in five modules in European style, which can be constructed separately in the workshop and assembled quickly with connecting screws.

The rear wall of the house was flat and uninviting. To make it friendlier, Hasenberg brought it down to "people scale." He shaped the family room as a series of one-story spaces and topped it with a low-pitched roof to avoid adding a third gable.

Broad steps merge deck with lawn.

"*We had this wonderful big backyard that was virtually inaccessible.*"

—**Russell Dow**

The new deck provides a sheltered outdoor play area for the kids within earshot of the kitchen and family room. Part of the deck stairsteps to the lawn, terminating in a six-sided landing that's just the place for Mom and Dad to chat or read while overseeing playtime activities below. The deck was built entirely of pressure-treated western softwoods. The planters were framed with foundation-grade lumber and exterior-grade plywood and sheathed with cedar shake siding.

132

More like an outdoor room, the two-level deck takes its shape from the new indoor spaces and the terraced terrain.

DESIGN FOR BUILT-INS: DAVE WOODS, DOVETAIL WOODWORKING. DESIGN FOR LIGHT FIXTURE: TOM FREEDMAN, CUTTING EDGE WOODWORKING.

An under-the-counter wine cooler serves the adult conversation area in the sun-room.

EXTRAS FOR GROWN-UPS

Twin built-ins frame the French doors in the sun-room. One set houses a wet bar plus glass-front cabinets for stemware. Base cabinets flank an Admiral under-counter cooler for Russell's wine collection.

The other built-ins include a writing desk with two sets of drawers under the work surface. Overhead, doors

Alexis' work area occupies a quiet corner in the sun-room.

with frosted panes camouflage shelving for books and supplies. The shelf units vary in depth to accommodate oversize items and lend architectural interest.

FINELY CRAFTED FINISHING TOUCHES

HIGH-TECH HANDLES

Drawers under the TV/VCR sport elegant, Oriental-style brushed-chrome bars mounted on black acrylic spacers.

ILLUMINATING ART

Airy grids crafted in Douglas fir (and treated with fire retardant) dress up store-bought pendants and sconces.

FINGER-PLEASIN' PULLS

Brushed chrome pulls on the media built-ins are user-friendly; their finger-fit forms offer a sure grip.

MULTI-COOK KITCHEN

DUPLICATE WORKSTATIONS KEEP COOKING DUO HAPPY

BY SUSAN SHEETZ

"We are basically two different types of cooks. I follow Julia Child, and Don is inventive."

—— Joan Beerline

"I clean up as I go along, and Joan doesn't. We wanted a kitchen that would function for two cooks."

—— Don Beerline

Photographs: Jay Graham. Design: Sandra and Barney Bird Custom Kitchens
Field editor: Helen Heitkamp

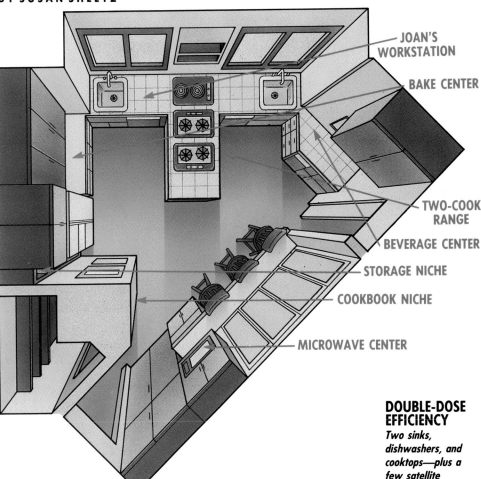

JOAN'S WORKSTATION

BAKE CENTER

TWO-COOK RANGE

BEVERAGE CENTER

STORAGE NICHE

COOKBOOK NICHE

MICROWAVE CENTER

DOUBLE-DOSE EFFICIENCY
Two sinks, dishwashers, and cooktops—plus a few satellite workstations—make for snag-free meal preparations.

Joan and Don Beerline are two avid cooks who love to share the kitchen but not cooking styles. Sound familiar? Then see how their double-up remodeling technique makes cooking together fun again.

135

BREATHING SPACE

"In the old kitchen," Don says, "Joan's 'mess' used to move across the kitchen counter toward me until I was squeezed into a corner."

"This kitchen was designed for serious cooks. We have our own crocks for spatulas, whisks, and spoons. The only thing we lack is a bulletproof curtain to pull down between us when we don't agree," chuckles Don.

▲MICROWAVE CENTER

The microwave center provides storage and serves as an eating bar, buffet table, and grocery landing space.

▲TWO-COOK RANGE

The peninsula was the key to the twin workstations and the only way for both cooks to share the range.

▲BAKE CENTER

Thirty inches grabbed from a bedroom closet rescaled the kitchen for the bake center.

"The individual workstations allow our son, Colin, and Don and me to cook together without invading each other's space," says Joan.

▲ JOAN'S WORKSTATION
With ample space between the range and the bake center, Joan can work at the range with a helper at the sink.

▲ BEVERAGE CENTER
A sliding-glass window lets Don and Joan pass food and beverages from the kitchen to the deck.

▲ COOKBOOK NICHE
A new cookbook niche (for the Beerlines' huge collection) and the ovens borrowed space from the old pantry.

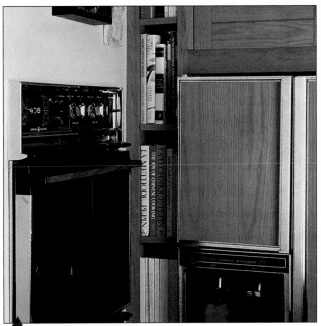

▲ STORAGE NICHE
The 7-inch space allowing clearance for the swing of the refrigerator doors provides bonus storage space. ▓

OCTOBER

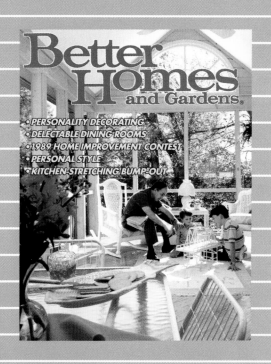

Better Homes and Gardens

- PERSONALITY DECORATING
- DELECTABLE DINING ROOMS
- 1989 HOME IMPROVEMENT CONTEST
- PERSONAL STYLE
- KITCHEN-STRETCHING BUMP-OUT

PERSONALITY DECORATING

BY SANDRA S. SORIA

Want to find a look you'll love to come home to? Don't follow fleeting design trends: follow your heart. Folks everywhere are getting personal with color, furnishing—style. The result? Homes that say who we are, not what we have. Meet three rooms that show you how.

SCANDINAVIAN SIMPLICITY

The Danielson family loves light, but they can't count on their Seattle climate. So they put their home in an ever-sunny mood with airy furniture and glowing backdrops.

A year in Sweden taught this family to see the light. They tore down curtains, rolled up carpet, and cheered up the home with white wicker and golden woods.

Bonny Danielson got out her needle and paintbrush to personalize the room. She quilted the pillows and painted the baskets that color this grouping.

PHOTOGRPAHS: LAURIE BLACK AND ROSLYN BANISH. DESIGN: JOSEPH P. HORAN. REGIONAL EDITOR: BARBARA EAST CATHCART

A white built-in bookcase adds the snap of contrast to brick-red walls, and shows off colorful books and objects from the owner's world travels. The red hue is woven around the room, linking objects of many origins.

ETHNIC ECLECTIC

A junk-shop chair reigns thronelike over a tabletop of treasures. Nubby linen fabric makes the carved-up chair compatible with the neighboring sofa.

Treasures found along the way bring wanderluster Joseph Horan's home to life. Set against warm red walls, the worldly objects, rich textiles, and mismatched furnishings compose a daring, one-of-a-kind collage.

TEX-MEX MIX

A western-style roundup of furnishings and accents whoop and holler about owner Melissa Fell's life and loves, which include horses, southwestern art, and kicking back. ▦

Earthy colors, touchable textures, and sink-in seating put guests at ease. Quirky accents—like the saddle and the feather bouquet—prompt a smile.

Lassoed with a belt and crowned with a hat, a cactus—and the corner—becomes as personality-charged as the rest of the wild, wild room.

DELECTABLE DINING ROOMS
SPICED WITH COLOR, FLAVORED WITH STYLE

BY SHARON NOVOTNE O'KEEFE

Sophisticated but never stuffy, these dazzling dining rooms invite lingering long after dessert. The secret ingredient? Each serves up a generous helping of personality.

CONVIVIAL COMFORT

In counterpoint to fast food and fast-paced living, these owners wanted the luxury of leisurely dining—not just on special occasions, but every day. The mealtime mecca they created succeeds with spirited color and soft seating.

Curvaceous and big on comfort, ample armchairs relax the mood and coax guests to dally over coffee and conversation. By day, the ebonized oak table hugs the wall, but, for entertaining, it takes center stage in the generous-size dining room. In this black-on-white setting, favorite art and captivating accents in eye-popping primary colors add lively finishing touches. Green-glass tent lamps glow over the table, lending French-café-style festivity.

PHOTOGRAPH: STEPHEN CRIDLAND. DESIGN: KAROL NIEMI. REGIONAL EDITOR: CATHY HOWARD

Bright accents and tableware add eye appeal in this high-comfort setting.

SAVORING TREASURES

Elegantly set to recharge body and spirit, this dramatic dining room is a visual feast of intriguing art and artifacts, sumptuous fabrics, and eye-catching furniture. Around the travertine-topped table, the shapely chairs, finished in matte black, are copies of an Egyptian design. The chairs' silk upholstery indulges diners and adds to the rich texture of the room's fabric mix. For bigger parties, canvas-draped side chairs move to a table in the bay window, where shoji screens maximize light and lend drama.

Collectibles were chosen for diversity, then pared to a chosen few for impact. Graceful pedestals, constructed of felt fabric over wood frames, hold major artifacts and punctuate the bay with interest. The parsons table sideboard holds Chinese obelisks, Portuguese greenware, and delicate crystal. Together, these worldly elements paint a personal portrait of the owner.

PHOTOGRAPH: LAURIE BLACK, ROSLYN BANISH. DESIGN: JOSEPH HORAN. REG'L EDITOR: BARBARA CATHCART

A world of artifacts, heirlooms, and art personalizes this dynamic dining room.

1989
HOME IMPROVEMENT CONTEST

YOU DID IT! *You met the challenge of our Home Improvement Contest. Your creative genius and boundless energies simply bowled us over. Here are the top-ranking projects, picked from a field of entries totaling more than 9,000.*

The tough part was deciding which entries to choose for prizes, because each had a great story to tell. We were right there with you as you ripped out walls, dug footings, and scraped paint. Nice work!

◀ **THE JUDGES:**
William L. Nolan,
Joan McCloskey,
Peter Mason,
Susan Sheetz,
Tom Jackson

THE WINNERS

1989

HOME IMPROVEMENT CONTEST

WHOLE-HOUSE MAKE-OVER

$11,000 GRAND-PRIZE

ELEGANT UPDATE FOR A '50s RANCH

"Our dream house has become a reality.
We learned so much, and it went so fast;
it almost makes you want to build
another house."
—CAROLYN AND WALT SWIATEK,
Burlington, Vermont

WINNER

▲ **GRAND-PRIZE WINNERS** Carolyn and Walt Swiatek check out the terrace with Jeff and Jennifer and Bear, their Bouvier.

◄ **GRACEFUL COLUMNS,** new windows, a canopied entry, and a larger second story transform the street side of this 30-year-old ranch in Vermont, updating it for the '90s.

We tip our hats to the Swiateks for giving their ho-hum ranch on Lake Champlain such a grand new lease on life. It's a winner, no mistake about it!

Initially, they planned a more modest revamp but raised their sights after architect Brad Rabinowitz sketched the home's real potential. "With this gorgeous location, to do less wouldn't have done it justice," say Walt and Carolyn.

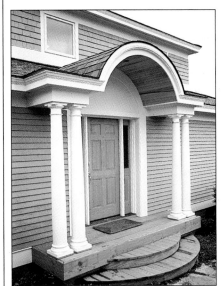

▲ **TWIN PAIRS OF COLUMNS** flank the arched entry canopy. Natural-finish beadboard warms the arch's underside.

WHAT THEY DID

● **Raised the roof** to make room for two bedrooms, a bath, and a den upstairs.

● **Installed new windows** throughout to let in more light and views of the lake.

● **Stretched the first floor** with a porticoed addition across the back of the house, a pavilionlike wing at one end. The rear addition adds space and light in the main rooms; the wing houses a private bath for the master suite.

● **Opened the main rooms up** to one another and vaulted the ceilings into the new rooms upstairs.

● **Upgraded the kitchen** with new cabinets and countertops (but kept their old appliances).

● **Restyled the exterior** with cedar shake and clapboard siding, Doric pillars, and an arched entry canopy.

● **Added a wet bar,** a screened porch, and a rear deck.

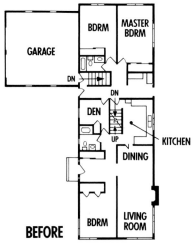

BEFORE

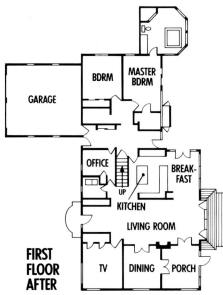

FIRST FLOOR AFTER

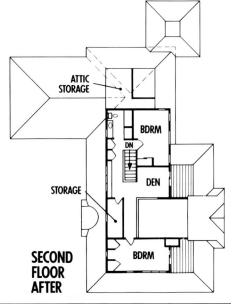

SECOND FLOOR AFTER

◀ **EXPANDING THE SECOND FLOOR,** adding a master bath wing, and stretching the main rooms downstairs took the kinks out of the old plan: a snarled traffic pattern and only one room for family activities.

Architect: Brad Rabinowitz. Project design: Betsy Sterling Builder: Herb Clement. Photographs: D. Randolph Foulds Regional editor: Estelle Bond Guralnick

146

▲ **STUNNING NEW STYLE!** White columns in the front hall frame the eye-popping living room. Tall windows in the new rear wall take in sweeping views of the lake.

▶ **STAIRSTEPPED OAK STRIPS** and a black marble hearth recast the fireplace in a deco mode. Inlaid parquet squares punctuate the corners.

"**All four of us are interested in cooking.
Everyone congregates here, so it's nice
to have that sense of openness.**"
— CAROLYN SWIATEK

Rabinowitz added square footage but preserved the home's earth-hugging silhouette. Comely arches cap the front entry and the rear window wall, and slim columns grace the garage wing and the terrace.

Eye-pleasing forms restyle the interior, too. Simple Doric columns flank the revamped living room; shapely windows brighten the breakfast room and

▲ BLUE TILES ADD a diamond pattern
underfoot in the breakfast room.

▲ GLASS-FRONT CABINETS showcase
Carolyn's blue-and-white china.

▲ A CURVY ISLAND
and a peninsula
cleanup center let the
new kitchen interact
with adjoining spaces
and the outdoors.
Upper cabinets hug the
inside wall, leaving
the view intact.

◀ NEW SQUARE
FOOTAGE IN BACK
houses the sun-
snatching breakfast
room. A beverage bar
next to the china
cabinet saves trips to
the kitchen.

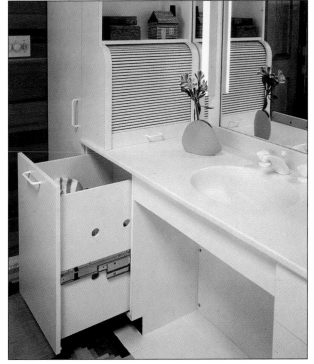

kitchen. Simple finishes flatter the forms: squares of black marble accent the deco-inspired fireplace, white beadboard dresses the breakfast room ceiling, and glass block zigzags around the tub in the master bath.

The bath occupies its own wing—another strategic add-on that upgrades the original plan. Now Walt and Carolyn have a private retreat at the far end of the house, complete with separate shower, walk-in closet, and panoramic views of the lake.

To escape the dust and din of the remodeling, the Swiateks rented a summer house nearby until the project was finished. This allowed them to keep costs in line by meeting at the site regularly with the architect, builder, and head carpenter. Total cost averaged $80 per square foot, typical for a major revamp. "We got good value for our investment," say Walt and Carolyn.

▲ A SERPENTINE GLASS-BLOCK WALL in the master bath zigzags around one corner of the spa, providing extra privacy for the vanity, shower, and toilet.

◀ BUILT-INS IN THE MASTER BATH include a drawer-style hamper and kneehole space under the vanity. Open shelving and an appliance garage keep towels and grooming aids within arm's reach of the sink. The garage's tambour door offers a quick cover-up for countertop clutter.

$1,000 FIRST-PRIZE INTERIOR

CREATIVE COMBINATIONS

CONTEMPORARY MEETS TRADITIONAL IN CONDO REHAB

"My husband prefers a modern European look. I have a penchant for antiques."

— KATHLEEN ASSER, New York City

▲ SOLOMON AND KATHLEEN stroll through Central Park with Tinker.

Busy schedules and spur-of-the-moment entertaining forged an uncommonly delightful alliance in Solomon and Kathleen Asser's plans for remodeling their condo.

Their low-upkeep lifestyle dictated clean-lined surfaces and built-in storage. The direct and simple geometry of the rooms, nonetheless, sets up a serene backdrop that highlights the Assers' traditional-style furnishings.

◄ THE DINING ROOM exemplifies the clean, low-maintenence look.

► UNCOVERED DURING the redo, the fireplace creates a cozy setting for traditional furnishings.

PHOTOGRAPHS: JON JENSEN. REGIONAL EDITOR: BONNIE MAHARAM. ARCHITECT: SOLOMON ASSER, AIA

◀ **A COOKTOP GRILL** in the new kitchen lets these city folk taste the great outdoors.

▲ **GLASS BLOCK** in the master bath provides privacy yet honors the open plan.

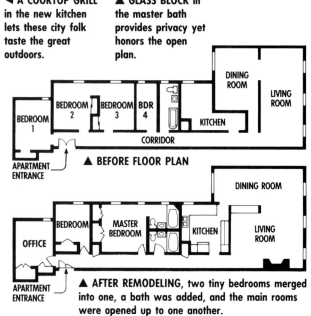

▲ **BEFORE FLOOR PLAN**

▲ **AFTER REMODELING,** two tiny bedrooms merged into one, a bath was added, and the main rooms were opened up to one another.

WHAT THEY DID

● **Rather than live with the dust and debris,** Solomon and Kathleen—like the Swiateks—moved out during the revamp.

● **Floor-plan changes** combined four small bedrooms into a master suite, home office, and guest room.

● **The Assers brightened the walls with paint,** replaced bath and kitchen fixtures, and installed new countertops.

1989
HOME IMPROVEMENT CONTEST

$5,000 GRAND-PRIZE RUNNER-UP
A CUT ABOVE THE REST
FINELY CRAFTED FAMILY BATH

▲ THE GEBHARDS TAKE A BREAK with Bran and Twig.

"To get the best value for our money, we paid as we went—and did it all ourselves!"

— CAROL AND GARY GEBHARD, Omaha, Nebraska

▲ BEFORE: POORLY PLACED FIXTURES and doorways.

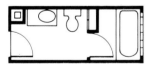

▲ AFTER: ROOM FOR A VANITY and a bigger tub.

It looks like a professional job, but Carol and Gary Gebhard did it all themselves (except the plumbing). Starting with a cramped, dreary, pink and green bathroom, they reworked the floor plan and vaulted the ceiling to generate extra roominess. Gary's woodworking talents contributed clean-lined built-ins and trim.

ARCHITECT: GARY GEBHARD. PHOTOGRAPHS: SCOTT LITTLE. REGIONAL EDITOR: MARY DIDIO

▲ EVERY INCH WORKS. Towels stow in a niche near the tub.

WHAT THEY DID

● **Relocated the fixtures** for more privacy and a smoother traffic pattern.
● **Removed one door opening** to gain precious wall space for the pedestal in the new tub room.
● **Added custom-designed built-ins:** a vanity, a linen cabinet, and a bench/towel niche.
● **Vaulted the ceiling** into the attic and popped in a skylight to gain more light without forfeiting privacy.
● **Crafted** a matching set of shoji-screen doors—from scratch!

▲ IN THE NEW PLAN, the sink and toilet are accessible from the hall when the tub is in use.

153

$1,000 FIRST-PRIZE KITCHEN

MADE TO MEASURE
A PERFECT FIT FOR TWO OR MORE COOKS

▲ **THE HIATTS.** Gina and Paul with Paul, Jr., 5, and Anna, 8. The whole family enjoys the new, wide-open kitchen.

> "We planned where everything was to go. We even measured for the height of the cereal boxes to be sure they'd fit on the shelves."
>
> — **GINA AND PAUL HIATT,**
> San Francisco Bay Area

Before Gina and Paul Hiatt even made a bid on their 19-year-old house, they consulted an architect to see if their kitchen remodeling plans were structurally feasible. They knew exactly what they wanted: a six-burner cooktop, two sinks, lots of counter work space for several cooks, and a sophisticated country look. After getting the architect's go-ahead, they bought the house and hired the firm to whip their murky galley kitchen into a paradise for a coterie of cooks.

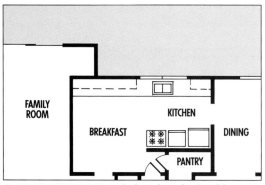

▲ **INEFFICIENT BEFORE.** A dark pocket of a breakfast room cramped the kitchen's style.

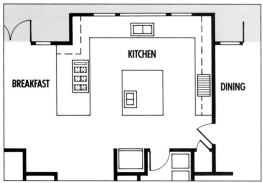

▲ **WIDE-OPEN AFTER.** The knock-down, bump-out redo lets the sunshine and cooks spread out in the space.

WHAT THEY DID

● **Bumped out** 8 feet from the back wall, added a big arched window, and knocked out a breakfast room wall.

● **Duplicated storage** and workstations with lots of counter space and a center island with a second sink.

● **Outfitted the island** with an ensemble of storage niches and pullouts for bakeware, lunch supplies, and fruits and veggies.

● **Installed a cooktop peninsula,** indoor barbecue grill, two sinks, and three ovens.

● **Used crown moldings,** paneled cabinets, 1×6 ceiling paneling, and period light fixtures for country style. Chose glass-fronted, mullioned overhead cupboards to echo the country flavor and ricochet light from the windows.

▲ **DISMAL GALLEY.** One window seeped a meager serving of light into the old kitchen.

▲ STORAGE HEAVEN. Pullouts galore keep bakeware and food fixings at hand.

▶ BAKE-CENTER BOOST. Gina's pullout step helps her wield the rolling pin.

▲ COOKS' PARADISE. Duplicate storage, sinks, and ovens keep a coterie of cooks happy.

◀ GLAMOUR GRILL. Marble tiles dress the indoor barbecue.

Architect: William B. Remick & Assoc. Photographs: Jay Graham. Illustrations: Mike Henry. Regional editor: Helen Heitkamp

▲ BEFORE REMODELING, the Thomases' no-space-to-spare bungalow had great views—if you stood on the roof.

▲ AFTER ADDING a second story, the family has room to expand and two decks for a choice of scenic views.

$5,000 GRAND-PRIZE RUNNER-UP

UPWARD BOUND
LIMITED LOT SPARKS SECOND-STORY ADD-UP

"Our children wanted their own bedrooms and we wanted a master suite. Nothing on the market suited our needs, so we decided to add on."

— MICHAEL AND JANET THOMAS, Seattle, Washington

There's only one place to go when the gettin' can't get better than what you got. Go up!

Blessed with a good neighborhood and the potential for great views, the Thomases' 78-year-old bungalow was nonetheless getting cramped. The tight lot ruled out a sideways expansion, so the Thomases put a second story on top.

This gained them a large bed-bath-dressing room, a study, a light court over the dining room, and an extra room for future expansion. Outdoors they added two decks plus roof framing for a future deck.

The new upstairs master suite frees up the downstairs bedrooms for the children and scoops up loads of daylight and solar warmth.

▲ MICHAEL AND JANET relax with Jennifer and Ben.

◄ SKYWARD REMODEL doubles the floor space. Open rafters on the end will cover a future deck.

▲ BEFORE REMODELING, four people crowded the single-story, two-bedroom cottage.

▲ AFTER REMODELING the first floor remains much the same, but with a deck over the garage in front and a stairwell.

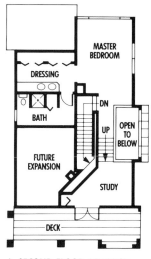

▲ SECOND-FLOOR ADDITION houses a master suite: bedroom, bath, and dressing room at one end, a study and deck at the other—plus room to expand.

"We started by taking out the ceilings and then it snowballed! This house was meant to be wide open so we could enjoy the view of the mountains."

— Michael and Janet Thomas

WHAT THEY DID

A narrow lot ruled out side additions, so the Thomases added a second story by tearing off the roof, building new walls on top of the old, and capping it all off with a new roof.

● **First-floor changes** were minimal. A deck was added over the garage and a staircase was built to the upper level.

● **New spaces created** included a tall light court over the dining room, a master suite, study, and upstairs deck. Additional space was reserved for future expansion.

● **Neighborhood character** was retained with the use of beveled siding, authentic divided-light windows, and a hefty, wood front door.

▲ **EXPOSED BEAMS** above the stairs leading to the study dramatize the space above the dining room.

◄ **THE MASTER BEDROOM** takes advantage of the roof profile with a triangular window.

◄ **WINDOWS** in the dining area stretch two full stories. The open space vents heat and pulls light into the house.

▲ THE CONANTS. David, Taylor, 2, and Cassie in a group hug.

$1,000 FIRST-PRIZE EXTERIOR

WEST COAST MAKE-OVER

FRESH FACE FOR A CALIFORNIA RAMBLER

"We took a dated ranch and created a home that's clean and classic. We like to think we gave it lots of character."

— DAVID AND CASSIE CONANT, Newport Beach, California

Homesick for their Wisconsin roots, the Conants wasted no time midwesternizing their unkempt California fixer-upper tract home shortly after moving in. They bounced ideas off an architect friend, then teamed up with a few good laborers. The fix-up left their home looking brand new—and increased its market value 100 percent!

▲ MIDWESTERN CHARM. Lap siding, peaked garage roof, and small-pane windows evoke Wisconsin roots.

▲ UNKEMPT BEFORE. Squabbling rooflines, tired trellises, and frowsy plantings were high on the cleanup list.

WHAT THEY DID

● **Ripped out** frowsy plantings, two trellises, rusted aluminum windows, and an entry overhang and half-wall.

● **Installed** French divided-light windows. Laid a new walkway and built planters.

● **Gabled** the garage roof and added dormers and flower boxes to the front windows.

● **Reroofed** with wood shakes and covered stucco with wood lap siding.

▲ WINDOW EXCITEMENT. Rusted aluminum windows gave way to eye-catching dormers and fetching window boxes.

159

$1,000 FIRST-PRIZE OUTDOOR

BUILT FOR BREEZES

PORCH AND DECK BRING IN THE GREAT OUTDOORS

▲ ENJOYING LIFE'S LEISURE in the fresh-air lane.

"We do a lot of cooking here, and it's where we eat on weekends."

— ANN AND BOB BAKER, Charleston, South Carolina

Ann and Bob Baker's new deck/porch addition gave them the best of both worlds—indoor comfort and outdoor fresh air. The floor-to-ceiling screens and gable window scoop in light and take advantage of the home's best backyard view. The screening also snares the slightest breeze while shutting out pesky bugs.

Windows in the house and a skylight over the porch entry help pull light and views indoors. The smooth threshold between the house and porch creates the feeling that both are part of a seamless whole. The attached deck provides a final transition from the house to the backyard greenery. ▣

▲ A BROAD DECK adjoins the screened porch, melding it with the house and the newly landscaped yard.

WHAT THEY DID

● **Angled** the door coming in from the deck. This kept the entry from eating up inside floor space.

● **Sealed** the pressure-treated pine porch floor with marine varnish to slough off wind-blown rain.

● **Used moisture-resistant gypsum board**, exterior grade, for the ceiling to give it a smooth, seamless finish that won't buckle, bulge or stain when exposed to outdoor moisture.

● **Wired** stereo speakers into the ceiling to bring music outdoors.

▲ THE GREAT OUTDOORS is part of everyday life on the Bakers' new porch.

*Muslin by the mile
sets an intriguing stage*

DRAPED FOR DRAMA

When decorating a room, feelings are as important as furnishings and frills. Here's how this owner put her living room in the mood for relaxed, carefree style.

Although preferences for period, pattern, and color are expressions of personal style, so are choices about what attitude your rooms convey. Ruth Draheim, a display artist from Seattle, clearly rebuffs crowded rooms, sharp edges, and hard surfaces. The result? A place that imparts a peaceful, easy-living feeling.

"I prefer simplicity over complexity," says Ruth. "But even though I like a room to be serene, I also like it to have a bit of 'pow,' a visual surprise."

Ruth's living room brings her philosophy to life. Spare without being Spartan and orderly without being rigid, it's an inviting and restful place. Under tossed-and-tucked dresses of unbleached muslin fabric, a daybed and chair have a dreamy look.

Lavishly and loosely applied, the muslin also "adopts" these unrelated pieces into the same furniture family. Muslin-covered cushions invite a bamboo chair into the fold, too.

Ironically, while the furnishings are draped, the windows are not. Instead, partially open miniblinds filter and soften both the light and the view. The sleek slats contrast the soft fabric folds for an eye-appealing change of texture.

As for the element of surprise, a blue lacquered coffee-table cube lends an island of cool contrast in a sea of creamy compatibility. It's a kind of bull's-eye around which the paler hued elements hover and revolve. "I don't like furnishings that seem to be cemented in place," Ruth says. "I'm forever fluffing

Muslin "robes" link a diverse grouping of furnishings.

A framed print and a clay pot crown a pale pine armoire.

Muslin curtains turn a once-dull hall into a dramatic passage.

and poofing and shuffling things; I think a room should be flexible."

Ruth's experimentation yields unexpected but delightful results, such as the doorway draperies between the dining and living rooms. The fabric adds privacy and discloses only a portion of what lies beyond, the way theater curtains gradually reveal a stage. Says Ruth, "All I did was cinch the muslin over a rod and let it fall to the floor. But it made the doorway seem grand—like a floor-length evening gown."

Photographs: Mike Jensen
Regional editor: Trish Maharam

161

favorites and new finds mix and relax

A CASUAL GET-TOGETHER

Furnishings enter and exit this room like actors in a play. The difference is, owner Joe McDonnal has no carefully thought-out design script; this room is inspiringly impromptu.

Floor plans, fabric swatches, and measuring tape don't figure into Joe McDonnal's scheme of things. Inside his 1903 cottage, rooms come together less by design than by desire. "To me, putting together a room isn't an intellectual thing," says the Seattle chef, "it's purely emotional. For the most part, these furnishings have appeared by happenstance."

Rather than chart out furniture purchases or hunt down just-right accessories, this homeowner led a quiet evolution. First, interior walls tumbled to reveal original columns. "I knocked down everything that could be knocked down," reports Joe. Having seen the light, Joe decided to further freshen the home's outlook with pale shades of paint, including a gray layer of enamel on the wood floors. "I love working with paint . . . ," he continues. "It's an easy and inexpensive way to give life to any room."

For this owner, another favorite character builder is fabric. Knowing that too much yardage and pattern can overpower a small space, though, Joe uses it with a light touch. Lending watercolor softness to the room's palette, simple cotton duck fabric freshens Victorian armchairs, wraps a bouquet of toss pillows, and frames a bay window.

The furnishings themselves have

Old and new, near and far come together in this worldly-wise living room.

Simple fabric foldbacks and painted import-store screens create an eye-opening window covering.

been paraded in from a variety of sources. The Victorian armchairs, for instance, landed in Joe's living room after being passed down by his mother. The carved window screens were hauled up from the basement, where they had been resting as dark wood floor screens. Cut down to size and painted gray, the lacy panels become intriguing sun filters.

Take stock of the other elements in this melting-pot place and it's clear that to this Seattle chef, a good room is like a good recipe: start with basic ingredients (airy backgrounds, a clean-lined sofa), then wake it up with a touch of the unexpected (prim chairs atop a dusky Turkish rug). The result will be familiar and comforting; the dash of surprise will make it unique. "I'm in favor of things," says Joe, "that exist for no other reason than to amuse you—bring you pleasure. I think that's a perfectly sound reason for being."

Photographs: Mike Jensen
Regional editor: Trish Maharam

BY SHARON L. NOVOTNE AND SANDRA S. SORIA

Feel-good accents sum up these owners' style

SHADES OF DIFFERENCE

Personal rooms are works in progress—ever changing to keep pace with evolving lives. This room opened a new chapter in a California couple's easygoing style.

As vivid as its cargo, a deep-blue-sea painted table puts treasured pottery on a pedestal for delightful display.

Pared to perfection, this simply serene room shows off eye-catching collectibles.

After organizing one great garage sale, Linda and Jim Matthews left their earthy browns-and-baskets period behind. Their destination? A spare-is-better setting that showcases the couple's enduring love of vibrant color, art, and aged pottery.

"We both realized we wanted something light, clean, and cheerful," explains Linda. "I love flowers, and I guess I wanted my house to be like the bouquets I enjoy—colorful, fresh, and unarranged."

Before the couple could start over style-wise, they first had to make hard choices in paring their accumulated collectibles and old furnishings. "Our tastes had evolved," says Linda, "so we decided to hang onto only what we truly loved. I sold $4,000 worth of stuff at the garage sale!"

Pottery of many colors, shapes, and vintages made the cut from old look to new, and remains Linda's collecting passion. "Color is usually the first thing that attracts me, but I also love the shapes, the finishes, and the versatility," says the collector.

Like characters on an ever-evolving stage, the richly hued pottery pieces move freely from room to room and from sofa table to dinner table—under Linda's direction. "It's fun when I set the table," says Linda, "and am able to share the pieces I've been collecting."

Against art-gallery-white walls, ceiling, and floor, the Matthewses' pottery and art collections become the main attraction. Furnishings are kept to a select few pieces, also subtly hued. Dressed in a nubby salmon-colored fabric, a modular sofa's ample size makes up for a lack of auxiliary seating pieces. "The room is big, so I wanted one mas-

sive and comfortable seating area," explains Linda. Floating in the center of the large space, the custom-designed seating forms an island of comfort.

For eye-pleasing balance to the soft seating, Linda added the clean-cut, richly grained Stickley child's table and rocker. Says Linda, "I fell in love with the table and chair for their simple lines—they'll last forever."

Photographs: Kim Brun
Regional editor: Sharon Haven

This home is an island of comfort in a sea of trees

A full-moon light fixture and a cool-gray wood stove add their own special glow to the deep-woods setting.

Hushed hues and marshmallow-soft seating compose a comfortingly serene scene in this rural home.

A SOFT TOUCH

Drawn to the woods for peace and quiet, a Seattle couple sought serenity inside their home, too. They found it in quiet hues, gentle seating, and natural accents.

Although tucked into the trees on an island in Puget Sound, this home hasn't succumbed to cabin fever. With nary a cedar plank, bear rug, or even a stone-studded hearth in sight, the easy-living room still offers deep-woods coziness—but filtered through city-slick sophistication.

Rather than pursue a well-marked rural route, Lee and John Paul Jones consciously chose a path less traveled when they designed their enchanting forest residence. "We wanted our home to be straightforward, but also unique," says John Paul, an interior designer. "I didn't want to follow any strong design trends and get trapped by clichés."

For one thing, the Joneses have created a setting that dares to be spare. Rather than fill the open living/dining area with lots of little pieces that fight for attention, this couple opted for a few, generously sized furnishings that rest the eye. "We wanted a feeling of spaciousness," says Lee. "To me, spareness and simplicity equal serenity."

Besides a lack of clutter, this room reflects a bold lack of color. White-washed walls, wood floors, and even fabric certainly soothe, but they can get cold as well. So, the Joneses turned up the visual heat with touchable textures and warming accents. Nubby natural linen dresses the focal-point sofas. Then, earthbound accents—such as paper lanterns and the twiggy floor screen—further rough up the place.

But the ultimate hot spot is the wood-burning stove. "That stove is an important part of the room," says Lee. "Even when not in use, it gives the connotation of warmth. It's primitive, comforting—something to gather around."

By keeping the furnishings hushed, the couple calls attention to the home's true star: its soul-soothing setting. Walls of glass blur the distinction between indoors and out, inviting the tall trees to be a part of the interior landscape. "We wanted the room itself to be subtle," explains Lee, "so that its real warmth and color would come from the woods, flowers, light, and people." ▦

Photographs: Mike Jensen
Regional editor: Trish Maharam

*Build character with
strong shapes and colors*

SENTIMENTAL JOURNEY

*Is it design savvy or simply
serendipity that melds an unlikely
mélange of furnishings and
accents into a room of matchless
style? For this owner, it's both.
Sure, she trusts her tastes, but
mostly she follows her heart.*

Richly layered and welcoming with a relaxed, old-world kind of charm, Donna Jorgensen's Seattle home speaks eloquently of her personal style. Every piece in this lovingly composed room has a story to tell—a tale, for example, of humble beginnings or transatlantic travels.

Take the spindle-back sofa. It was about to be orphaned by a friend, when Donna adopted it and gave it a snappy white linen dress. The worldly-wise textiles were residing in a dusty, British antiques shop when Donna discovered them while on vacation there. Gathered together, personal pieces such as these give a room a warm-all-over, happy-ending feeling.

"All the pieces have in common is that they were rescued. I tend to find pieces I love in haphazard places or get them from friends; then I refurbish or recycle them if they fit," Donna says. "I guess loving all of them makes them good company to one another—at least in my eyes. A little paint never hurts either."

Walls coated in a deep, rich red embrace Donna's favored furnishings like a warm hug. Because a lot of heavy color can appear more gloomy than glowing, Donna lightened the room's complexion with high-luster white architecture, a white ceiling, and a bleached wood floor. "I love the deep red color," explains Donna. "All day long, light changes the quality of the room."

Set against a rich red backdrop, found-along-the-way treasures and timeless textiles create a signature look.

Spiffed-up seating and a lyre-based table join love-at-first-sight accents for warm and charming, sentimental style.

The medley of pattern and texture adds to the room's warmth and wealth of character. For instance, Donna collects paisley shawls and other aged textiles to add subtle pattern and soft touches throughout the room. When draped over the back of an old chair, paisley fabric lends off-the-shoulder elegance. Nearby, another pinch of pais-

ley is tossed atop a canvas-covered table and set warmly aglow by lamplight. Bamboo shades, a better-for-wear area rug, and a rose-chintz chaise are drawn into the mix by their earthy colors and textures.

But the true ties that bind the room's entire cast of characters are the owner's heartstrings. Donna explains her "let it be" philosophy: "For me, the room's richness comes from putting together pieces, fabric, and colors that appeal to me," says the homeowner. "I think if you see a piece you can't live without, it will end up being at home with the others. Gradually, my intuition tells me if I need a change in color or placement. Once the pieces have landed and work in my eyes, then I stop fussing."

Photographs: Mike Jensen
Regional editor: Trish Maharam

KITCHEN-STRETCHING BUMP-OUT

MAKING ROOM FOR FAMILY AND FRIENDS TO GATHER

Bumping out 5 feet onto a concrete patio slab and letting in a large dose of sunlight enriched this kitchen with hospitality.

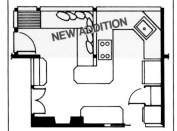

Room for a crowd

When family and friends gathered in the old, 7×15-foot kitchen, the room seemed crowded. An extra 5×17-foot space, with large windows facing the steeply sloped, ivy-covered backyard, lets everyone breathe, mingle, and enjoy the view.

The banquette welcomes kitchen visitors.

Custom interior

The homeowners gutted the existing kitchen and built a U-shape work area with custom oak cabinets. The addition of a breakfast counter, planning desk, and banquette transformed the room into a comfortable center of activity.

Efficiency

The homeowners chose to keep the food preparation area compact and efficient, using the extra space for other functions. The informal eating counter doubles as an auxiliary kitchen counter during parties and extended family gatherings. In the banquette area, a south-facing glass door opens to the backyard. The cost of remodeling was about $15,000.

New eating counter and desk fill existing kitchen space.

The U-shape work area extends into bumped-out space.

PLAYFUL PAINTED PIECES
HOW TO MAKE THEM; WHERE TO GET THEM

Lighthearted and childishly delightful, painted furniture stars as an artful accent in today's homes. Here's how to search out—or whip up—a piece of your own.

BRUSHING UP

You can create your own off-the-wall masterpiece—even if you don't have fancy brushstrokes. Try your hand at simple shapes—squares, triangles, or circles—like the design on the revved-up, secondhand desk chair (*right*). And remember, relax and be creative! After all, you can always paint over your "mistakes." Use quick-drying acrylic enamel paints. Paint a base coat; let it dry. Try various colors and brushes to compose your own freehand designs.

Against a painted and stretched canvas, this chair becomes an eye-popper.

WHERE TO BUY PAINTED PIECES

Look for painted furnishings at local art galleries, crafts shops, and home specialty stores. More mail-order catalogs featuring high-quality accessories are selling such items, too. Expect to find accents—mirrors or decorative boxes—as well as major furnishings, including armoires and tables. Many artists also will paint pieces on commission. Search out an artist through local galleries or art schools.

LIVING WITH ART FURNITURE

When using art furniture, limit yourself to one or two pieces per room so that every piece is a standout. Display each as you would a painting: against a simple, uncluttered backdrop. ▧

HEAVENLY BATH
TRANSFORMED BY A MAGIC WINDOW

A favorite antique, heirloom, or white elephant can turn out to be the focal point that ties a remodeling project to your existing house. Alan and Wendy Goer started with an aged window beauty.

The antique window sets the tone and color scheme for this master bath.

THE MAGIC WINDOW

Put a stained-glass window in your master bathroom? Why not. In converting a large hall closet with window to a master bath in their 1860s home, the Goers set the room's vintage tone and its color scheme by replacing the old double-hung window with a stained-glass antique.

FOCAL POINT

The celestial glow of the window provides light and privacy in the street-fronting bath. At night, the window doubles as a unique, backlighted painting on the home's exterior.

Wendy repeated the window's pastel colors in the wallpaper, carved synthetic ceiling molding, ornate mirror frame, vanity, and bathtub tile. The window's ribbon motif reappears in the wallpaper and ceiling molding, too.

The tub/shower and laminate vanity are contemporary concessions.

OLD-FASHIONED MERGER

The modern-day tub/shower unit and Corian-topped laminate vanity merge unobtrusively into more old-fashioned surroundings. These include the diamond-patterned ceramic floor tile, deep baseboards, and glass-fronted medicine cabinet. ▧

SLIDE-AWAY STORAGE

VERTICAL DRAWERS MAKE A SLICK MEDICINE CABINET

By Susan Sheetz

MATCH THE WOOD and drawer pulls with your existing cabinetry.

Here's a different "slant" you might consider for solving a familiar small-bathroom problem: too-little storage space.

A clever twist

When is a drawer a cabinet? When you mount it vertically on the wall. Turning it on end nets more room for your medicines and toiletries than many mirror-front medicine cabinets provide. Our example measures just 6½ × 45 × 22 inches. Build it in a weekend or two, then watch clutter disappear in your bathroom.

Pointers

● Divide each drawer into three sections: one 4-inch compartment on top, one 5-inch compartment on the bottom, and an 8-inch compartment in the middle to accommodate a variety of bottle and box sizes.

● If you run the track hardware along the inside back of

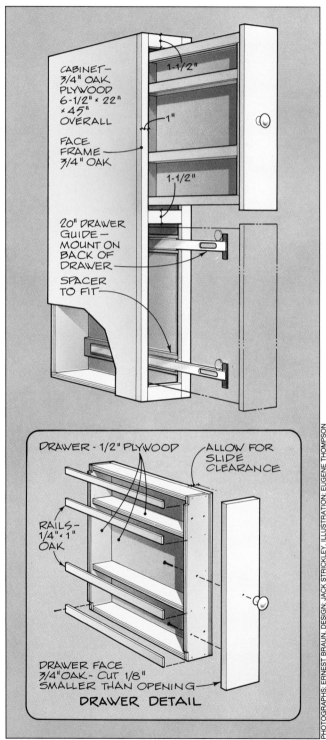

CABINET—
3/4" OAK
PLYWOOD
6-1/2" × 22"
× 45"
OVERALL

FACE
FRAME
3/4" OAK

1-1/2"

1"

1-1/2"

20" DRAWER
GUIDE—
MOUNT ON
BACK OF
DRAWER

SPACER
TO FIT

DRAWER - 1/2" PLYWOOD

ALLOW FOR
SLIDE
CLEARANCE

RAILS—
1/4" × 1"
OAK

DRAWER FACE
3/4" OAK - CUT 1/8"
SMALLER THAN OPENING

DRAWER DETAIL

TWIN DRAWERS stack inside the wall-mounted cabinet. The ¾ × 1½-inch rail on the right edge of the cabinet was used to keep the drawer from bumping into the door trim.

SHELF RAILS keep medicines and such secure "in transit."

the cabinet, mount it before you anchor the side of the cabinet to the wall. Run the glide hardware along the back of each drawer.

● The drawer should be 1 inch narrower than the opening to allow for the glides and tracks.

● The face of the drawer should be ⅛ to ³⁄₁₆ inch smaller than the opening. ▦

DRAWER GLIDES are mounted on the tops and bottoms of the cabinet and drawers.

MASTER-SUITE SPA
A RETREAT TO SERENITY

PHOTOGRAPHS: KARLIS GRANTS. ARCHITECT: CHARLES SCROGIN. FIELD EDITOR: CATHY HOWARD

A view from the master bedroom to the spa, a converted atrium.

A soak in the whirlpool tub is the final step in the O'Hollarens' daily exercise routine. As their muscles relax in the warm swirl, the surrounding beauty of the space helps ease their minds.

SOLVING A PROBLEM

A 20×20-foot open-air atrium, with glass walls on three sides, was the centerpiece of a spacious master suite. "It was lovely at first," says Susan O'Hollaren, whose home is in the Pacific Northwest, "but it collected a lot of moisture and moss, and it required too much maintenance."

Converting the space to a luxurious spa not only solved the maintenance problem, but created "a year-round source of pleasure," says Susan. "We use it as our own very private retreat."

HOW THEY DID IT

The first step was to pour a concrete floor and then lower the tub into place using a crane. The couple can service the whirlpool motor from the basement. Next came the ceramic tile floor and, finally, double-paned skylights. The door to the spa opens from the small den connected to the bedroom.

Looking back to the bedroom. Good ventilation prevents steamy windows.

WELL VENTILATED

An air-to-air heat exchanger vents humid air and brings in fresh air from outside—minimizing condensation on the glass panels. In the winter, the exchanger extracts heat from outgoing air and transfers it to incoming air. In summer, the direction of the heat exchange is simply reversed to cool the spa area. A plastic pool cover conserves heat when the tub is not in use. 🔳

CATCH THE WAVE
WATERBEDS ARE BETTER THAN EVER

COURTESY OF WESLEY ALLEN

Surprise! This bygone-era resting spot is really a modern-day waterbed.

Once considered a passing fad, waterbeds have floated into the mainstream. Now, waterbed buyers pick from a sea of types.

WATERBEDS MAKE A BIG SPLASH

Waterbeds have come a long way. Though the bag-and-boards model still exists, a new soft-sided waterbed is now popular. In the new type, the water mattress is encased in rigid foam and topped with quilting. These flotation systems look like conventional mattresses and use standard linens.

What's more, these lighter weight, hybrid waterbeds fit a variety of frame styles, such as the nostalgic brass bed (*above*). Some makes, such as the "Cashmere" by *Somma*, feature individual tubes that you simply carry to the sink and fill.

Modern waterbeds also offer varying degrees of motion. "Full motion" provides a rocking effect, "slow motion" is calmer, and a "waveless" model is nearly still. Cost varies from $200 to $2,500 depending on make and degree of motion (less is more).

BUYING TIPS

When shopping, be certain the:
- **MATTRESS VINYL** measures at least 20 millimeters thick.
- **WARRANTY** covers materials and construction for five to 10 years.
- **HEATING UNIT** bears a UL label, designating a safe electrical system. 🔳

NOVEMBER

Better Homes and Gardens

- FIVE GREAT LOOKS FROM FIVE GREAT GALLERIES
- WIDE-OPEN KITCHEN REDO
- SMALL-SPACE BATHS
- COMFORT COMES HOME

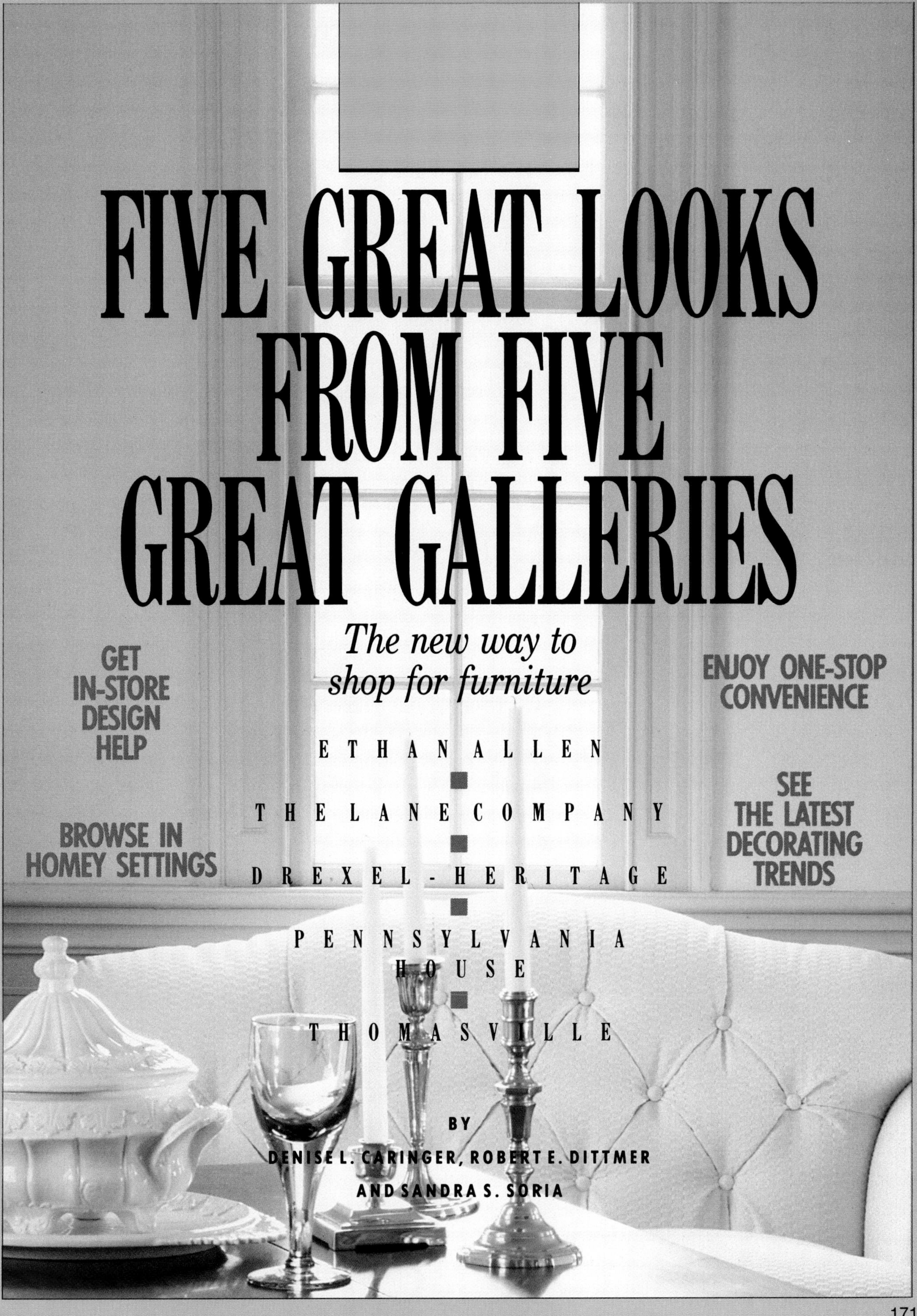

FIVE GREAT LOOKS FROM FIVE GREAT GALLERIES

The new way to shop for furniture

GET
IN-STORE
DESIGN
HELP

BROWSE IN
HOMEY SETTINGS

ENJOY ONE-STOP
CONVENIENCE

SEE
THE LATEST
DECORATING
TRENDS

ETHAN ALLEN

THE LANE COMPANY

DREXEL-HERITAGE

PENNSYLVANIA HOUSE

THOMASVILLE

BY

DENISE L. CARINGER, ROBERT E. DITTMER
AND SANDRA S. SORIA

FARMHOUSE FLAVOR

OK, so there's no rooster, but you can almost hear one crowing in the distance, can't you? As if tinged with the first light of day, golden pine pieces cast a sunny glow no matter what the hour. Team these kitchen classics with black wing chairs and a checked floor, and you have a hot spot for that first cup of coffee or late-night snack.

ROOM PHOTOGRAPHS: JON JENSEN. FURNITURE PHOTOGRAPHS: TATUM, TOOMEY & WHICKER

At galleries such as Ethan Allen (the maker who opened the door to the gallery concept), you'll stroll through a mix of homey room settings until you find a style that invites. These pine pieces beckon with down-home charm.

ETHAN ALLEN

■

URBAN COWBOY

*Forget the usual skins-and-bones desert look; this room gets
its trendy southwestern flavor from kinder, gentler elements. The
sofa—its chunkiness and hardy checks give it rugged appeal—joins
with south-of-the-border-inspired metals for a robust look that's
at home on the range or in suburbia.*

THE LANE COMPANY

As pearls top off an evening dress, accessories turn a plain room into a polished one. Galleries help you choose a room's "jewelry" by showing complete outfits—from rugs to artwork.

THOROUGHLY MODERN MING

Got a yen for oriental drama? Satisfy it fast. Instead of a family of oriental pieces, let one bold individual, like this entertainment unit, set the mood. Pull up a couple of contemporary chairs and a coffee table (oriental, like this one, or a modern glass-topped version), then settle back and flick on the TV.

Afraid to blend eras, nationalities, even patterns in your place? Turn to a furniture gallery, where you'll find design help, a complete menu of furniture styles—and the confidence to create a look all your own.

177

SHOPPING THE FURNITURE GALLERIES

CHERRY JUBILEE

*This unexpected blend of breezy, natural wicker with stately
18th-century cherry proves that opposites not only attract—they're attractive!
The tie that binds: the wicker's mellow, antiquelike finish. Want to give
formal furniture a more casual character? Simply add fresh, blooming
fabrics and a few easygoing pieces.*

PENNSYLVANIA
HOUSE

You'll be exposed to classic furniture design as well as up-to-the-minute merchandise at today's galleries. Many sets show how to blend the best of the past and present. So, you can relax, browse, and be inspired.

FRENCH DRESSINGS

Timeless shapes and antiqued finishes imbue these Gallic furnishings with old-world flavor. Use one handsome piece, like the upholstered, open-arm lounge chair, to give your place a foreign accent. Or, immerse yourself in continental antiquity with a roomful of matching French dining pieces.

What will the best-dressed rooms be wearing this year? Count on the galleries to keep you up-to-date on the latest furniture and fabric fashion trends. This French country look isn't revolutionary, but it is oh-so-chic.

THOMASVILLE

WIDE-OPEN KITCHEN REDO

HARMONIOUS MIX OF OLD AND NEW

BY SUSAN SHEETZ

AIRY AND BRIGHT. Eighteen recessed lights supplement lots of natural window light.

Your kitchen could be right on target—for the needs of a bygone era! Andrea and Craig LaBarge's update of their 1925 kitchen may spark some ideas on how to get the '90s style you need and want.

TRANSFORMING THE PAST

"In the '20s, the residents of old-world-style homes like ours didn't gather in the kitchen," says Andrea LaBarge. "The kitchens were designed for the equipment, not the people."

Andrea yearned for a big modern kitchen that would allow her to entertain without isolating her from family and guests. But she still wished it to fit in with the rest of her English Tudor home. "We wanted a warm, traditional feel as opposed to a slick, high-tech look," she says.

Cramped space gave way to big and open.

KNOCKING DOWN WALLS

The LaBarges first gutted a warren of four dark rooms, including a butler's pantry and the obsolete kitchen. This opened up a 20×30-foot area.

Then they turned to St. Louis interior designer Danean Mitchell to help them get the most use from this large room. Her response: one bright, flowing space with four loosely defined areas: kitchen, bar, dining, and entertainment. And she opened it to the outside brick patio with elegant French doors.

WORKING WITH RESTRICTIONS

A chimney and a chase column that contained the plumbing and projected more than a foot from the wall were two major design challenges. Danean enclosed them, creating space for

LOOKOUT POINT. From the preparation island, the cook has a clear view of guests or family—as well as the media wall—in the free-flowing room.

the wall cabinetry below the windows. She also provided a clever bonus: a wine rack at the end of the chase column's extension of cabinets.

"In the '20s, . . . the kitchens were designed for the equipment, not the people."
—Andrea LaBarge

The new kitchen angles into one of the corners of the wide-open room, and a preparation island mimics the angle.

The L-shaped island gives the cook a multitude of refreshing views during meal preparation. It is also a multipurpose marvel: Two marble landing spaces hold hot dishes, and a second sink provides a quick-rinse area for

SITTING AREA PLUS. A former butler's pantry now houses the TV, VCR, and stereo behind sleek cabinet doors.

both produce and pots. The combination gas and electric stove tackles heat-and-eat and slow-cook dishes at the same time. Cook's helpers can gather at the two-seater snack bar.

TRADITIONAL TIE

Teak flooring, with its appealing warmth and texture, brings a touch of formality to the room. Andrea loves the crisp blue-and-white striped wallpaper, both for its traditional English feel and the clean, fresh, contemporary edge it gives the kitchen.

As you update your behind-the-times kitchen, keep this remodeling strategy in mind: A careful blend of traditional design with '90s style can offer the modern conveniences you crave and let you keep treasured features of the past.

SMALL SPACE BATHS

BY
WILLIAM L. NOLAN

These three minibaths live big by making every inch count. A deft blend of line and light lends big-bath glamour—a formula that works for *any* small bath!

TRADING THEIR TUB for a shower suited the Cuffaros' kids just fine (they hate tub baths). Bands of blue tile with contrasting edges tie the shower stall to the vanity countertop.

Photographs: Joan Vanderschuit. Design: Steven Doctor. Regional editor: Sharon Haven

CORNERING SPACE FOR KIDS

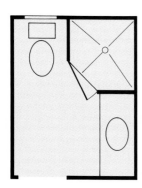

Original fixtures left the Cuffaros' vintage 6 × 7½-foot bath looking crowded and cluttered. Their two boys prefer showers, so Joe and Kathy traded the old tub for a corner-hugging shower. This scheme produced bonus floor space plus ample room for a 4-foot-wide vanity. To gain wall space for the shower, they shifted the bathroom window to one side and tucked the toilet under the windowsill. A clear glass shower door and a large mirror give an added boost to the bath's new roominess.

SMALL SPACE BATHS

HIGH-GLOSS materials ease cleanup and lend urbane polish. The Schunks chose glazed tile for the walls, glass block for the window and shower enclosure, terrazzo for the floor, and black laminate for the vanity.

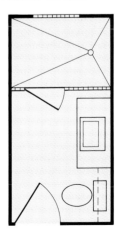

NATURAL LIGHT FROM the shower window spills into the room through transparent glass block. Deco-style sconces mounted on the big mirror over the vanity seem to float within the glass-block grid.

RETOOLING AN OLD STANDARD

Jan and Carl Schunk's 1912-vintage bath aped a standard 5×7-foot fixture layout—toilet and pedestal sink along one side, a tub spanning the end wall under the window, and no space to spare for a shower stall. Simple changes transformed the space. A roomy shower stall replaced the tub, visually extending the floor all the way to the end wall. A giant mirror expands the room's dimensions, doubling the apparent depth of the laminate countertop and the glass-block shower walls.

SMALL SPACE BATHS

CLEAR GLASS DOORS merge the room-for-two shower stall with the rest of the bath, letting light spill through from the glass-block wall in back. Soft shades of gray in the ceramic tile help the end walls to recede.

MIRRORS OVER THE vanity sheathe a bank of shallow cabinets above the twin lavatories. Separate compartments hold grooming aids, Sarah's jewelry, and Scott's ties.

ACCOMMODATING HIS AND HERS

Tight siting left a scant 8×8 feet for the bathroom in Scott and Sarah Chipman's master suite addition, not much room for two people getting ready for work at the same time each morning. Clever built-ins and a streamlined plan headed off bottlenecks, and neat tricks with light yielded visual stretch. The tub-size shower alcove sports twin shower heads, one at each end. Glass block lets the alcove share light from the bedroom windows; mirrors over the vanity magnify the light inside the bath.

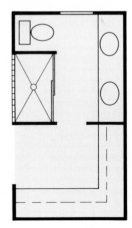

COMFORT COMES HOME
WAYS TO WARM UP A DECORATING SCHEME

Set to soothe, this warmly personal place takes heart from vintage midwestern treasures—then gets its soul from settle-back comfort. Come on in and learn its decorating secrets.

A ROOM WITH ROOTS

This beckoning Oregon living room offers the warmth of country without the clichés. In place of the loom and gloom of dark, dominant furnishings, you'll find cozy-up colors, friendly finishing touches, and a select few, beautiful and dutiful antiques. The elements compose a portrait of the owner: a transplanted Midwesterner who followed her heart to create a room she loves to come home to.

AT-EASE ELEMENTS

Curl up by the fire, kick off your shoes, and relax. It's a house rule in this welcoming family retreat. Then, take these comfort cues to "relax" your hardworking rooms:

● **Pillow-plumped sofas** dressed in country-style cotton fabric face off at hearthside. The fabric recalls yesterday's homespuns and links the cozy contemporary seating to other aged elements in the room.

Glowing woods and cotton-clad seating calm this sun-washed living room.

An old tricycle enjoys elevated status as primitive sculpture.

● **Walls softened with a hint of blue** lend a restful feeling to the room. Oriental porcelain accents and the wall-hung quilt's bold pattern carry the blues around the space.

● **Golden-grained accents** impart character but deliver up-to-date function. A generously sized library table serves as an unexpected sofa table, ample for showing off such favored pieces as the charming old tricycle.

● **A variety of touchable textiles,** including a cozy new rug, the vintage quilt, and a homespun coverlet, add lively punches of color throughout the space. The stitchery also offers a soft counterpoint to the antiques' rich woods and the mellow oak flooring, to visually awaken the room.

REVEILLE FOR RELICS

More than just pretty faces in this easy-living scheme, favored collectibles report for duty in a variety of cleverly cast roles. Timeworn toolboxes and an old dough bowl, for instance, serve as convenient caches for books and magazines. A better-for-wear wooden pail blooms with bouquets from the homeowner's beloved perennials garden. And the room's complement of lamps consists of electrified "finds," such as old crockery and a mismatched selection of English candlesticks. ▩

DECEMBER

_____
_____
_____
_____
_____
_____
_____
_____
_____
_____
_____
_____
_____
_____

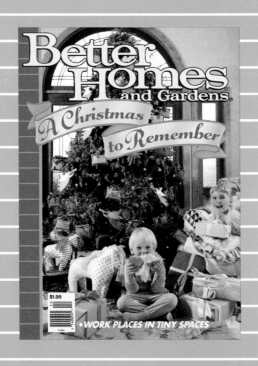

_____
_____
_____
_____
_____
_____
_____
_____

WORK PLACES IN TINY SPACES
WHERE A LITTLE ROOM GOES A LONG WAY

BY ANN HINGA KLEIN

PHOTOGRAPH: JAY GRAHAM. DESIGN: ANNIE BOWMAN, SUNRISE INTERIORS. REGIONAL EDITOR: HELEN HEITKAMP

The detachable table in this home office makes way for overnight guests.

In search of a place to call home office? Don't give up for lack of room. Here are furnishings that make work places of tiny spaces.

WORK ZONE

A pint-size room can manage a home office if given the right furnishings. The detachable worktable (*above*) tucks under and out of the way when patio traffic picks up. Its teammate? A smart storage unit that shoulders more than its share of the workload, offering shelves and drawers for art objects as well as office supplies. The neutral color and contemporary lines of these *Techline* pieces lend impact to Windsor chairs and country cushions. This space also offers a fringe benefit: the sofa unfolds into a bed for overnight guests.

NEW LIFE FOR DEAD SPACE

Even a narrow slice of space makes a handy candidate for office detail. Originally a walk-in closet, the nook (*below*)

PHOTO: SUSAN GILMORE. REG'L EDITOR: B. BACZYNSKI

Ingenious indentations keep workhorses from snarling TV traffic in this work-and-play space.

is now a natural for paying bills and keeping household files. A custom-cut, laminate work surface curves inward so chairs won't block traffic. Underneath, metal file cabinets offer support and hold documents. White wire closet shelving welcomes books and accessories in style. Beyond the desk, inexpensive futons provide a ready rest stop, while an exercise bike stands ready for workouts when the paperwork is done.

MAKE WAY FOR HOME WORK

Still stumped in your search for a workstation? See if your laundry room and kitchen crannies can accommodate the compact pieces shown here. Or, put a dining room to work on weekdays, then simply send the typewriter packing when you unpack the china. 🏠

189

INDEX